WORKING WOMEN

Working Women

THE SUBTERRANEAN WORLD OF STREET PROSTITUTION

Arlene Carmen and Howard Moody

 A Cornelia & Michael Bessie Book

HARPER & ROW, PUBLISHERS, New York
Cambridge, Philadelphia, San Francisco, London
Mexico City, São Paulo, Singapore, Sydney

FIRST EDITION

Designer: Sidney Feinberg

This book is set in 10-point ComCom Gael by The Haddon Craftsmen, Inc., ComCom Division, Allentown, Pennsylvania, and printed and bound by The Haddon Craftsmen, Inc., Scranton, Pennsylvania.

Library of Congress Cataloging-in-Publication Data

Carmen, Arlene.
    Working women.
    "A Cornelia and Michael Bessie book."
    1. Social work with prostitutes—New York (N.Y.)
2. Church work with prostitutes—New York (N.Y.)
3. Prostitution—New York (N.Y.) I. Moody, Howard.
II. Title
HQ316.N6C37   1985   362.8   84-48585
ISBN 0-06-039040-9

---

85 86 87 88 89 HC 10 9 8 7 6 5 4 3 2 1

Dedicated to the memory of Bonnie, Judy, Slim, Barbara, Jenny, and all those women we never knew who lost their lives violently, and for whom change in society's attitudes and laws will come too late

Contents

Acknowledgments

We want to thank all those whose cooperation and forbearance made this book possible. All of them know who they are even if we don't mention their names.

First, a special thanks to the women of the streets, who because of their trust and belief in us opened their lives and made it possible for us to discredit the bad press and dispel some of the untruths and distortions. We thank them particularly for their prose and poetry included in this volume.

We need to express our gratitude to the congregation of Judson Church, whose support and encouragement of the Prostitution Project made our involvement and immersion in this world possible—particularly those who drove the mobile unit and prepared food for serving to the women, and the women from our church who early on joined Arlene in her street watch in areas of public prostitution. Special gratitude to Essie Borden for her care and competence in typing the manuscript.

Introduction

This book was written to record experiences, observations, and the evolution of attitudes in some eight years of direct work and relationship with New York prostitutes. It is not a psychological analysis of women who are working prostitutes; several of those have already been written. It is not a sociological book based on objective data culled from questionnaires. It is not a historical review of how prostitution grew up in different periods. Rather, it is a book based on existential involvement with the life and world, both private and social, of street prostitutes in New York City. It is impressionistic, a particular and personal document about a group of women engaged in the business of recreational sex. Though it is written by outsiders from another "world," it is partisan and empathetic to those "working women" whose lives are made more miserable by their being forced into the illicit subculture of criminal activity.

There is no claim that prostitution in other cities, states, or nations is the same as depicted here. This picture is purposely parochial, confined to a single stratum of prostitution (streetwalkers) in a single locale.

If this book has any distinctiveness in the literature concerning prostitution, it lies in the perspective and posture of the writers. Most books about prostitution and prostitutes are written from what claims to be an "objective" and "analytical" point of view. Most books (and articles, for that matter) written about prostitution from a sociological point of view approach the subject as a phenomenon of "social pathology" in which prostitutes are seen as helpless victims of antisocial pathogens who choose to act out their rebellion against normal societal patterns or are forced by economic needs to settle for "the life."

Other books, written from psychological perspectives, tend to view prostitution as a mental "sickness" or "deviancy" that requires therapeutic treatment to avoid crippling emotions and psychological self-destruction. This view is limited, and seriously distorted, by its basis in a middle-class norm for sexual activity, and in the fact that therapists see only prostitutes who are remanded by the system, or come voluntarily because they are disturbed by what they are doing. (There were a lot more homosexuals going to psychiatrists before the American Psychiatric Association removed the label of "sickness" from the lifestyle of gays.) Therapists seem not to realize that the prostitutes' misery stems in large part from what society tells them they are —"sick and deviant"—and their desire to be acceptable and normal human beings. Their sexual immaturity, parental rebellion, and adolescent tribulations are no different from those of the rest of our society, but we judge more harshly the forms their "growing up absurd" take.

Anyone who has any experience existentially and socially with the abortion issue, or with homosexuality, will recognize the role the social establishment (therapists, teachers, preachers, social workers) played in writing the self-fulfilling prophecy of "sick" and "disturbed" that those men and women felt as a result of what they were doing and who they were.

The writers of this book do not claim to be objective. As a matter of record, we went into this work with many prejudices taught by our society. In all honesty, we came out of the experience with a different impression, and with perceptions that challenge most of the popular mythology about prostitutes and the subculture they inhabit. For us, a serious question mark has been posited to society's attitudes and the punitive laws by which this minority in our culture is judged and punished.

Let us explain what we mean by "subculture." When anthropologists took up the study of urban culture, they looked at certain ethnic enclaves, some particular neighborhoods to be dissected and analyzed. But when we speak about "the life," the world in which prostitutes live, we are talking about something different, what someone once called "niches in the mind, and in the psyche of the city." An urban subculture is not a group of people living in a certain village or neighborhood, but a set of norms that is different from those of the broader culture— a body of rules, a world view, a way of looking at life. The people may be scattered all over the landscape, but they identify with each other because they *share* a particular set of norms. When we use the word "subculture," that's what we are describing. As we immersed ourselves in this subculture, the nature of the life unfolded, correcting our misconceptions, exposing our prejudices, and calling into question some of the values of our dominant culture.

If from time to time in these pages we philosophize about the women's plight or compare their morality with our own, or probe our judgments about the women's life-style for their inconsistencies, it is in order to illumine the views and attitudes of the dominant culture in our society—i.e., white and middle class. We are not trying to disparage the values of our own class, but rather to test the constancy with which we apply those values to everyone.

How we view people and problems determines in large measure how we deal with them. We also acknowledge that these women and the problem they pose for our society may not be the most significant or most immediate social issue facing us, but it does seem that their story is worthy of telling; the place we have assigned them worth noting; and the punishment we have meted out to them worth questioning.

WORKING WOMEN

Working Women accurately depicts our experience with the Judson Church Prostitution Project.

However, in mentioning people connected with "the life," real names have not been used and we have altered street names, individual characteristics, and locales to protect the identities of those involved.

1

Prolegomena to Times Square

They come in all sizes and colors
Black, Spanish, White, and others
Tall, short, fat, skinny, and even out of shape
Yes, yes, gentlemen, all to satisfy your taste
On sale at a corner near you
Anywhere in New York you choose
Whether it's uptown, downtown, or midtown
We're getting down everywhere in this town
Thiefs, freaks, flatbacks, and sleaze
Choose as you please, from any of these
Ladies of the night.

—ME

The misty rain, chilling the late-night air, washes the dirty streets of the Times Square area, and people move briskly up Eighth Avenue to avoid the cold. The neon calling cards of marquees begin to flicker out, giving the streets the appearance of semidarkness. The street habitués congregate in front of a steel-gated darkened movie house, silently conversing with passersby in the sign language of the street hustler. Squad cars prowl silently like hunting dogs sniffing the air for their prey, and then periodically the call of the wild streets pierces the night and the screeching banshees alert every denizen of the street that the hounds are in pursuit. Then just as quickly as they screamed their presence, it is quiet again. The crowded streets are beginning to thin now, people who sought their pleasure in movies, theater, and dining are bustling home. And those who are on the streets for business suddenly appear, as if on cue for their nightly debut, along with those who have no place to go and nothing to do but watch the unrehearsed choreography of this shadowy netherworld, another kind of street theater, where people play their roles, buying and selling the illicit "sins" of the city: a banned play of staged criminality where all participants know their part and act it out—police and prostitutes, junkies and narcs, muggers and the anticrime squads, fences and bargain-hunters. It is a symbiotic drama in a Stygian world where everybody lives off one another's vices and vulnerabilities. This masque of the mean streets is for spectators with strong stomachs and a taste for black comedy and outrageous irony.

As the lights go down on the avenue and the drama unfolds, the chief protagonists in the late-night show in Times Square, as in every place in the world where this "immorality play" is seen, are the "women of the night"—prostitutes, those purveyors of recreational sex, those caterers to bodily appetites. Their star quality comes from the strange ambivalence that the simultaneous attraction and repulsion of their presence evokes in us, and we have a vague sense that they have played this role for several millennia, in every kind of setting and civilization. Older than a Greek chorus, as new as the latest chorus line, the prostitutes continue in their roles to entice and infuriate us.

Whether or not prostitution is "the world's oldest profession," it clearly is one of the most persistent and universal social issues in the history of both ancient and modern cultures. It would be folly to look at Times Square, or Eleventh Avenue, or Lexington, or Delancey Street, and pretend that what we are seeing is some new city problem left over from the last administration for our present mayor to clean up. Sometimes we talk and act as if this were true, but in our sober moments we know that we are dealing with but one aspect of the issue of human sexuality in our modern world. And it comes to us laden with the baggage of the moral, legal, and social sanctions that are its historical legacy. It is not our task here to dissect ancient history, but it is hoped that in order to understand more fully this sexual phenomenon, the reader will pursue some of the excellent studies that have been done in recent times.*

For our purposes, here is a very cursory and synoptic history of prostitution in America. It may seem somewhat excessive to claim that like violence, prostitution, far from being a foreign import, is "as American as apple pie," and has been with us in all its varied manifestations since the beginnings of this country.

It has been said that in the colonial period, America did not have much prostitution, not because of any moral rectitude or legal sanctions, but simply because there wasn't much need for it. Adultery and fornication were so prevalent as to render the issue of prostitution secondary or insignificant. The acknowledged promiscuity of prominent persons like Benjamin Franklin (who wrote a ribald essay called "Advice to a Young Man in Choosing a Mistress," not published but freely circulated) and Alexander Hamilton is an indicator of the level of tolerance in the eighteenth century, that mythological paradise of puritans and pietists, who ironically have about as bad a reputation among modern liberals as do pimps and prostitutes. That period of American history seems to foreshadow the Victorian attitude of passive toleration of prostitution. It was condemned but not criminalized; hidden away but not dramatized. Prostitution was seen then as St. Augustine had described it, a "necessary evil," but not as a social evil to be punished by society's law.

Before there were any laws against prostitution, and before the reform era in the late nineteenth century, social disapproval and attacks upon prostitutes were carried out by indignant citizens with the help of rowdy gangs and billy clubs. There were spontaneous and rather unorganized mob attacks upon bordellos, called "whorehouse riots," which were com-

Perspectives on Prostitution, by Jennifer James, Debra Boyer, Jean Withers, and Marilyn Haft (Seattle, Wash.: Judicial Advocates); *The Lost Sisterhood: Prostitution in America, 1900–1918,* by Ruth Rosen (Baltimore: The Johns Hopkins University Press, 1982); *Deviant Street Networks: Prostitution in New York City,* by Bernard Cohen (Lexington, Mass.: D. C. Heath, 1980).

mon to urban areas. The houses were burned down and many times the rioters fought with police (who at that time were probably the women's paid protectors). Despite these sporadic and occasional outbursts of righteous indignation, the "Victorian" attitude prevailed: Prostitution was necessary. Keep it quiet, keep it hidden, and let it live. But that toleration was to change in the mid-nineteenth century.

At that time there came two waves of migration in this country—the westward migration of Americans and immigration of poor Middle Europeans into the cities of the east coast. Contradictory ways of treating prostitutes resulted. In the great western migration, the so-called bordello grew to a stable and accepted institution in every prairie town, along with church, saloon, and school. The cattle towns and gold rush towns were peopled by men without women, and prostitutes were tolerated, much as they were—and for the same reasons—by St. Augustine in the Roman Empire of the fifth century. They served as protection for the few married women who were citizens of the town. Prostitutes were accepted in the West, and they contributed to the building of churches and hospitals and to campaigns of civic improvement—the legendary whores with hearts of gold.

At about the same time that prostitution was becoming acceptable, if not respectable, in the West, a quite different view of prostitutes was growing in the cities of the East. With the Middle European immigration, there came the first overt prostitution in the street. Men who had left their women in the old country were here in great masses, and they craved sex. Many of the European women who migrated to the large cities found it preferable to work at prostitution than to labor in the horrendous sweatshops and factories.

If you listen to Clinton neighborhood people or Lexington Avenue citizens or the Mayor's Task Force wax indignant, you would think that New York, along with other American cities, has reached a new nadir of vice and sin. But city cleanup campaigns go back a hundred years. "There is no city in the world where there is so much vice, so many entirely abandoned and reckless women," lamented one journalist after the Civil War. By 1870, there were 10,000 prostitutes in a city of 950,000 people, according to several newspaper estimates. As one contemporary writer puts it, "A hundred years ago—as today—society hypocritically tolerated prostitution as long as it was discreet, out of the way, and tainted with shame. But once these activities came out into the open and were easily available to more than just the very rich and very poor, society suddenly saw itself besieged by a wave of vice and sin." (Charles Lockwood, op-ed page, *New York Times,* 4/10/70.)

Unable to endure the poor's buying and having sexual pleasures in the same way the upper classes had always had them, the white Protestant establishment mounted a moral crusade against the beer-drinking, loose-living immigrants who threatened the dominant culture patterns. Cleanup campaigns were waged with passionate moral indignation. This led to the closing down of brothels, a cracking down on street prostitution, and finally, as well, to Prohibition. All these crusades were not necessarily a commentary upon the morality of good and upright people; rather, they were an exposure of class prejudice and discrimination. In other words, if you have worked hard, have saved some money, you can have a mistress or visit a "house of ill repute," but if you are poor and are forced to buy or sell sex on the street, it is a threat to the morals of society. Things haven't changed much, when you consider that a call girl operating out of a luxury East Side apartment in New York City experiences no censure, while a poor black woman who uses the streets to find her customers is the target of harassment and punishment.

If you will pardon a little historical déjà vu, the nineteenth-century streetwalkers of lower Broadway offered a similarly easy target of vice drives. During the city's 1855 foray among the unhappy women who perambulated Broadway, Trinity

Church vestryman George Templeton Strong confided to his diary that "what the Mayor seeks to abolish or abate is not the terrible evil of prostitution . . . but simply the scandal and the offense of the peripatetic whorearchy. He is . . . trying to keep vice from proclaiming its allurements in the market place. The great notorious ladies' boarding houses of Leonard and Mercer Streets are left in peace." (Ibid.)

It is important to note here that there were certain historic factors in this "Progressive Era" that played an important part in the rise and spread of street prostitution.

First, there was the reformers' crusade to close down and abolish all brothels and the red-light districts that had grown to house this large invisible and illicit trade. When these were closed, there was no place but the streets for the poorer women to go. The logic that if you closed down brothels you would drive prostitutes to the streets seemed to escape the avid reformers of the nineteenth century, and it escapes them today. The more massage parlors and prostitution hotels you close down, the more women are out on the streets, where their visibility antagonizes other citizens.

It is important to understand that in the large urban areas in the period 1850–1900, prostitution in brothels and red-light districts was both tolerated and protected by politicians. Large and prominent districts like the Tenderloin in San Francisco and Storyville in New Orleans could not have flourished and survived without the explicit knowledge and assistance of big-city politicians, who in exchange lined their political coffers with payoffs and bribes, the "friendly extortion" of those mutually engaged in illicit activity. As a matter of fact, when the reform movement to clean up the cities and abolish prostitution gained momentum in the early 1900s, many a politician found himself defeated by charges of his protecting his city's red-light district.

Of course, politicians could not have protected the brothels without the help of the police, who were paid off handsomely and took their orders from the political incumbent. The continuance of prostitution required the compliance and corruption of police departments. Bordellos and districts paid unofficial "fines" in order to maintain "services of protection." Prostitution, great commercial enterprise that it was, made a lot of the respectable very wealthy. But the reform movement in the first part of this century put an end to that, and politicians and police turned from being the protectors of prostitutes to being their prosecutors. With the breakdown of "houses" and "districts," individual prostitutes out on the street became the victims of harassment by police and condemnation by politicians. America was changing, reform was in the saddle, vice was being opposed openly, and the prostitutes were victims of this movement. But history always has a way of affecting our morals, and new events were to shift our attitudes once again.

During World Wars I and II, there was a tremendous upsurge in prostitution around base camps and in towns near large military installations. Once again the tolerance grew because "men were without women." (It is a testimony to our sexist society that the same kind of concern was never shown for "women without men.") In both the Korean and the Vietnam wars, prostitution was tolerated and controlled. In South Vietnam a special brothel was built at Ankhe, exclusively for American soldiers. A senior medical officer suggested in 1969 that brothels be run by the military post exchange system, but his idea was never acted upon.

Following World War II, there were increasingly liberal attitudes concerning sexual mores, obscenity, and pornography in practice, while laws against and punishment of prostitutes continued and in most instances were increased. Today we are faced with the most ambivalent attitudes yet toward sexual mores and prostitutes. One cannot look at prostitution in America except in the larger context of our attitudes toward sex generally, and it is in that context of society's toleration and even demand for sex that our attitude toward prostitution is seen to be most flagrantly ambiguous.

Now, one of the ways we have tried to rid ourselves of prostitutes is by making laws that forbid their doing business. The problem with legal sanctions against prostitution is: (1) they don't work—arresting, fining, and jailing seldom stop a prostitute from working; (2) almost all of the laws are unconstitutional; and (3) all of them are highly discriminatory—only women are prosecuted, and most are streetwalkers, who in most cities are black and poor.

In regard to the effectiveness of antiprostitution laws, it seems obvious that criminal sanctions, as a matter of historical fact, have not stopped prostitution. The "cleanup campaigns" of New York City for the past hundred years have not abolished prostitutes. If the law were effective in ridding the streets of prostitution, one might find a rationale for the warped priorities of police chasing women and letting real criminals strike at will. Any honest politician who cared about real crime would make law enforcement's top priority the prevention and detection of violent crimes against people and property.

But even though the laws against prostitutes don't seem to mitigate the practice, neighborhood groups keep pressuring the police to get rid of them.

How come they hate us so? We ain't doin' nothin' to them. Yesterday I'm just standin' on the corner, not doin' nothin', and this bitch come by and says, "Get off the street, you dirty slut." If she hadn't been so fast I'd have kicked her ass. I wasn't hurtin' her. Where does she get off, callin' me names? You mean to tell me she ain't never fucked for favors? We just tryin' to make a livin' like everybody else.

More important than the pragmatic argument is the one of principle that most antiprostitution laws are fundamentally unconstitutional. We submit this opinion on several grounds that have been established in cases before the courts. The prostitute's rights are violated on the grounds of freedom of (1) speech; (2) privacy; and (3) equal protection. Most antiprostitution laws that seek to control the trade forbid not the *act* itself but *soliciting* for it.

Regarding the question of free speech, in most laws it is the solicitation itself, the exchange of words, that constitutes the offense. The issue is whether the words used by the prostitute ("Hey, honey! You wanna go out?" "You want a date?" "Do you want to have a good time?") "are used in such circumstances and are of such a nature as to create a clear and present danger, that they will bring about the substantive evil that rises far above public inconvenience, annoyance or unrest" (*Terminello* v. *Chicago* 337 U.S. 1 [1949]). Because free speech is so important in a democracy, we tolerate a lot of offensive and uncivil speech in order to protect that right. And of course we are all selective in what we find obnoxious. Every day on the streets of the city, women are subjected to men's verbal sexual advances and off-color remarks, and though it is offensive and degrading to most women, and is even intolerable to those who overhear it, there is no public outcry to make this form of speech criminal. Furthermore, on the street we are continually subjected to annoyances by panhandlers, peddlers, Hare Krishnas, and religious fanatics.

Statutory proscription of prostitution and all other sexual activity between consenting adults would appear to be constitutional invasion of the rights of privacy. Yet the Supreme Court has almost consistently thrown protection around personal intimacy and bodily integrity. In a decision handed down eighty-five years ago, there was an eloquent expression of this principle:

> No right is held more sacred or more carefully guarded by common law, than the right of every individual to the possession and control of his own person free from all restraint and interference by others

unless by clear and unquestionable authority. (*Union Pacific Railway* v. *Botsford* 141 U.S. 250 [1891])

In more recent times, another famous case reiterated and reinforced the rights of privacy, singling out sexual privacy in particular (*Griswold* v. *Connecticut* 381 U.S. 479 [1965]).

We also find that most of the language of the antiprostitution statutes and nearly all the enforcement of the law are highly discriminatory. This is in spite of the fact that there is practically no difference between the conduct of the prostitute and that of the patron. A New York City court observed almost fifty years ago:

> The men create the market, and the women who supply the demand pay the penalty. It is time that this unfair discrimination and injustice should cease. . . . The practical application of the law as heretofore enforced is an unjust discrimination against women in the matter of an offense, which in its very nature if completed requires the participation of men. (*People* v. *Edwards* 180 NYS 631,634–5 NYC Ct. [1920])

Things have not changed much. In spite of the change in the language of a few state statutes, the antiprostitution laws remain both in substance and in practice the most blatant example of sexism in law enforcement, and a clear and consistent violation of the equal protection clause of the Fourteenth Amendment. The male patron and the female prostitute are equal partners in commercial sex; there is no legitimate distinction between their conduct.

The idea that a woman can commit an act of prostitution only by selling her services to a man perpetuates the myth of the "fallen woman," which has largely shaped societal responses. By consigning the female prostitute to a class by herself, society creates a voluptuous icon who becomes the collective scapegoat; her punishment becomes her atonement, and it exonerates those whose participation in her brand of sin is less visible. As with all scapegoats, her symbolic status blocks any perception of her role and her rights. We remember Audrey, who, with lips trembling and voice filled with outrage, told Arlene how "Crazy Beast" (a plainclothesman) had physically abused her because she wouldn't identify "her man" in the rogues' gallery prints. She showed the knuckles on her hand, which were covered with scabs: "Crazy Beast" had knocked her down and then stepped on her hand, grinding her knuckles into the cement. She said he had also taken money from her.

In regard to all these matters, then, the antiprostitution laws appear highly unconstitutional. But even so, there is something more morally reprehensible and legally unjustifiable that is part of the daily practice of law enforcement—namely, that a woman who is labeled a prostitute and so known by the police may be arrested, incarcerated, and fined not for any crime she is guilty of committing but simply for *who she is.* We remember Tiffany, sitting in a diner having her evening meal. The diner was full of working women and non-street people. A policeman came in, pulled her off the stool, and ran her in, booking her for soliciting for the purposes of prostitution. Paula, who lives near a prostitution area, tells of going for groceries for her children, when the police threw her in a patrol car and booked her at the precinct house. There is no class of persons, with the possible exception of those labeled "Mafia," whose rights and legal protection are so blatantly ignored as are prostitutes'. The Supreme Court has already decided that despite the risk that narcotic addicts may rob or mug someone, or on occasion even kill, merely *being* an addict is not sufficient reason for a person to be arrested and incarcerated. But still prostitutes are arrested every day for nothing more than *who* they are. It is a dangerous precedent in a land of liberty and freedom. Periodically, people are arrested not for who they are but because they *look* as if that's who they are. Women not prostitutes, who stand or walk in a place where prostitutes congregate, may be arrested for soliciting because they appear to be one of "them."

In order to do justice to those who disagree with the premise regarding the unconstitutionality of our antiprostitution laws, let us address their arguments. Such people believe there are "substantive evils" that justify the curtailment of the rights and liberties of prostitutes on behalf of the larger good of society; that indeed there are circumstances in which individual freedom may be abrogated. (The Mafia, with its criminal network of illegal activity including murder, constitutes such an exception.) The justification runs like this: When the state has a compelling reason for violating the constitutional rights of a citizen, it may adduce a balancing of freedom and order. Those who defend the presence and strict enforcement of antiprostitution laws do so on the grounds that there is a "compelling state interest," which lies in three areas: (1) public health; (2) public safety; and (3) public morals. Once again, the mythology regarding prostitution and the damage it causes to society is as pervasive as it is unsubstantiated by any real facts, but the laws are based on lore and not on facts. Even a cursory look at each of the three areas will show how weak indeed is the argument for "compelling state interest."

In regard to public health, the contention is that prostitutes spread venereal disease. All the recent sociological and public health studies show that the VD rate among working prostitutes is very low. In a comprehensive study of prostitutes, Dr. Jennifer James of the University of Washington Medical School concludes that "Public Health advisors believe that the increase in venereal disease is related more to a general change in sexual values unaccompanied by health education" ("Prostitution in Seattle," *Washington State Bar News*, August–September 1971). Dr. William Edwards, chief of preventive medicine in the Nevada State Health Division, agrees with the contention that the problem is not in the house of prostitution but in the general population. He indicated that the rate of VD among prostitutes is less than 5 percent, while among high school students aged fifteen to nineteen the rate is 25 percent (*Honolulu State Bulletin*, March 23, 1972).

It will come as no surprise to women in "the life" or people who have any experience with "the life" more immediate than media imagery or textbook sociology that the rate is so low. It is low not because the activity of the life is not highly susceptible to the contact and spread of disease, but because the prostitutes are smart enough to know this and wise enough to take extreme preventive measures. Over and over again the women stress their uncompromising attitude toward sex of any kind without condoms.

Sally is laughing at the naïveté of a trick earlier in the evening:

Man, that asshole thought just because I was giving him a blow job he didn't need no rubber. I told him no way, honey, you gonna have this mouth around that cock les'n you have a rubber. I don't give a damn if'n the mothah is the President; he's gonna wear a rubber. No siree—no rubber, no blow. Take it or leave it, but don't waste my time.

It is this street smartness about prophylactics that makes the VD rate so low and unwanted pregnancies among prostitutes the exception rather than the rule, and assures the "rubber man" an exceptionally good moonlighting business.

Dr. Charles Winick, in his book *The Lively Commerce* (Quadrangle, 1971) states that most studies show VD attributable to prostitutes in this country to be somewhere between 3 and 5 percent of the total. If we want to protect the public from the spread of venereal disease, which has reached epidemic proportions in certain areas, it is clear from the facts that stopping prostitution altogether will have little effect on that threat to our public health.

A second "substantive evil" invoked for outlawing prostitution is that this "lively commerce" is tied to organized crime, or to put it another way, prostitutes attract criminal elements wherever they go. This is another part of the lore that dies hard.

Most of the recent studies on prostitution deny any supportable evidence of connections with organized crime. The reasons given for this range from the fact that the business is not lucrative enough, to the observation that prostitution is too visible for organized crime to be connected with.

It is not as clear that there are not underworld connections with the pornography industry (movie houses and porn parlors), just as there was, and in some places still is, a serious involvement of organized crime in gambling and the jukebox business. The Presidential Task Force Report on Organized Crime speaks to this issue:

> Prostitution . . . plays a small and declining role in organized crime's operations. . . . Prostitution is difficult to organize and discipline is hard to maintain. Several important convictions of organized crime figures in prostitution cases in the 1930s and 40s made criminal executives wary of further participation. ("Crime and Its Impact—An Assessment," The President's Commission on Law Enforcement and Administration of Justice [Washington, D.C., 1967])

It seems that prostitution, at least as practiced in New York City, is one of the last bastions of small, free-enterprise, laissez-faire capitalism. Pimps are independent entrepreneurial businessmen, each with his own rules and regulations, and women without pimps virtually defy collective organizing. It seems far from certain that prostitution has been infiltrated or has ties to "organized crime," but if it were proved that such was true, would we favor the abolition of prostitution? If so, why not close down casinos in Nevada or outlaw certain labor unions? *If* the Mafia underworld were trying to muscle in on the prostitution enterprise, would it not serve the purposes of the law to try and convict and punish the agents of organized crime rather than abolish prostitution? When gambling is made legal, the state makes every effort to keep "known criminals" out, but it doesn't close down casinos and arrest their owners.

Now, as for the charge that prostitutes attract and are the

cause of ancillary crime, this is demonstrably a specious argument. In the first place, if prostitution were not itself a crime, the chances of its attracting related criminal activity would be much less. Wherever society insists on creating criminal subcultures (gambling, homosexuality, drugs) by making certain social activities illegal, the people from various strata of this illicit underworld gather together to feed on each other's fears and phobias, reinforcing their criminal behavior both in jail and on the streets. Furthermore, there seems to be little solid evidence that so-called related crimes that follow open solicitation for the purpose of prostitution can be attributed to prostitutes themselves, with the possible exception of "rolling a trick." Thus it is even more unjustifiable to arrest and prosecute a prostitute because of the *possibility* that some unidentifiable ancillary crime might be involved. From one court decision addressing the issue of the prohibition of protected behavior to prevent possible related harms:

> A State may no more prohibit mere possession of obscenity on the ground that it may lead to anti-social conduct than it may prohibit the possession of chemistry books on the ground that they may lead to the manufacture of home-made spirits. (*Stanley* v. *Georgia* 394 U.S. Ct. 566 [1969])

Finally we come to the last of the three areas in which the state contends it has a compelling interest to protect the public, and that is public morals. The morality question permits even less substantial proof that prostitution is a threat. We hear all the time that prostitution is injurious to a neighborhood or community—that, for example, it is injurious to children who see this "seamy" side of life. We all know that our children see more immoral and obscene things, such as murder, rape, and racism, on the evening news than they could ever view walking on the "stroll" in Times Square. There is an interesting observation in an article on prostitution in the United States and Europe:

Even at the Salvation Army's Amsterdam headquarters, adjacent to the red-lighted windows, the women and their work are accepted as a fact of life. Lt. Col. A. M. Bosshardt, the Army's chief social worker, is not agitating to close prostitution down, but counsels the women and estimates that she helps about fifty a year who want to leave the profession. To her the proximity of families and brothels in the same neighborhood is not shocking. "No children from this district go into prostitution. They see all the bad sides." A psychiatrist who has studied young prostitutes gives his opinion about the effect on children living in the area: "Cigarette smoking is more dangerous." ("The Biggest Pimp of All," by Elizabeth and James Forenberg [*Atlantic Monthly,* January 1977])

Underlying this claim about bad influence is the conviction that prostitution both is immoral and undermines the stability of the family. Regarding the first belief, the state is on dangerous ground if it relies upon the mere assertion of immorality to justify a criminal prohibition.

As for the threat to family life, we consider the argument that prostitutes are a threat to the stability of the family to be a highly dubious construct, even though it is true that the most frequent patrons of prostitutes are married men. A telling judgment on this question was issued by Judge Margaret Taylor of the New York City Family Court:

If the State's objective is to promote the stability of the family, and it contends that commercial sex has a direct impact upon the family, then the law should focus on the conduct of the patron. However it has never been demonstrated that commercial sex has had any effect on the stability of marriage or the family. Indeed, although prostitution has been practiced for centuries, disruption of the family has never been causally related to prostitution. (*New York Law Journal,* January 23, 1978, p. 12)

And further, it is certainly far from evident that in those places in Europe and the U.S. where prostitution has been decriminalized and/or legalized we have seen any damage or marked deterioration of family life.

In this brief treatment of the legal issues underlying prostitution, the antiprostitution advocates have inadequate if not flimsy rational evidence for depriving prostitutes of their right to work unmolested by and protected from police and tricks and pimps. The truth of the matter is that society finds a woman performing recreational sex for money "objectionable" and "immoral" and seeks ways of justifying the prohibition of this sexual commerce, but no objective reading of the facts can substantiate that commercial sex threatens harm to our public safety, health, or welfare.

So we are back to Times Square, trying to understand the century-long cleanup of the territory. We still use the language of "morality," which we translate to "crime," and we try to save a woman from her "sin" by locking her up. But these moral shifts and slides simply reveal the relativity of our ethical norm.

We were reminded very concretely about this by a wonderfully good-humored philosopher–bar owner on Eighth Avenue in the midst of the open prostitution area. His little bar and restaurant (now closed) catered to pimps and prostitutes, and regularly he was harassed and condemned by the police and his neighbors because he served this "human garbage." At one point his indignation reached the boiling point, and he reminisced about his eighteen years' experiences as a café owner, and the changing fads in morality. He remembered the early sixties, when his place was a hangout for homosexuals. He served them and treated them like human beings while being castigated by the police and his neighbors for serving these moral outlaws. "Today 'those people' can eat and drink anywhere and other people are fighting for their civil rights. And now they tell me those prostitutes and pimps shouldn't be able to drink and eat in my place. C'mon, get off my back. People got rights—who's gonna be tomorrow's scapegoat?" Who, indeed?

Times Square is not just a geographical location; it is a state

of mind, a piece of culture, a slice of life transferable in space
and time to medieval London, sixteenth-century Rome, Paris in
the 1920s. It is many places in many times: wherever the
voyeurs of forbidden sights, the seekers of erotic delights, the
hunters of bodily revels gather in these hunting grounds of
illicit leisure. There, when the rest of the city closes up and
darkens down, this arena opens, frightening in the variety of its
lures, perplexing in its confusion of the illegal and the illicit. Its
characters change with time—yesterday's moral outlaws are
today's solid citizens, yesterday's peeping-tom emporiums
today's forbidden palaces. The unchanging attraction of these
locales are the prostitutes. How we were lured into their corner
and enticed to travel into their underworld is a complex story.

2

Culture Shock: Entry into Another World

> In all reality women of the night life struggle to survive in a world of anxiety, so there shouldn't be any disrespect in return for their justification of their life. For everyone should have an understanding for you and I.
>
> —BUTTER

Prostitution was far from our minds in 1975, consumed as we were by a life-or-death struggle to save the Center for Reproductive and Sexual Health (CRASH), the first and largest ambulatory abortion clinic in the United States. After years of running the Clergy Consultation Service on Abortion, which counseled and referred women for what was then an illegal medical procedure, Judson Church had been instrumental in the founding of CRASH in 1970, when abortion became a woman's right in New York State. We hoped it would be a model for the delivery of abortion services in a humane and caring environment, and it fulfilled that expectation.

Then suddenly, in 1973, the U.S. Supreme Court struck down abortion laws throughout the land and the weekly patient load at CRASH tumbled precipitously from eight hundred to fewer than two hundred. Management, unable to retrench, went into debt, and the CRASH board of trustees, acting with great speed, decided to close the clinic, sell its assets, and pay their bills. At this stage we intervened, appealing to the board for an opportunity to salvage CRASH. It was foolish, sentimental, and unrealistic, but reflected our deep attachment to a place that had served thousands of women from all over the country at very low fees, and whose existence had demonstrated to the hospital-oriented bureaucracy of New York City's Department of Health that not all medical procedures require general anesthesia, two days in the hospital, and a huge bill.

That the not-for-profit world sometimes resembles the fairy tales of our youth was reflected in that board of trustees. They acceded to our request, resigned en masse, and elected in their place a new board composed of members of the congregation of Judson Memorial Church. For the two years that followed, all energy was devoted to saving CRASH; rarely did we allow ourselves to dream of ways in which 25,000 square feet of beautifully designed and furnished space might be used for innovative women's health services. Focused on survival, we had no time for the luxury of fantasy.

This changed abruptly in 1975 when Howard Moody was invited to a small meeting of political activists at the home of philanthropist Stewart Mott. There he met a woman who was a former prostitute, attempting to organize a union, Prostitutes of New York (PONY). She talked about a need among that population for decent gynecological services. She claimed that the small group of Manhattan physicians who cared for the health needs of women in the profession exploited them medically, financially, and sexually. She was looking for an alternative, and it seemed not unreasonable to consider undertaking that task within the walls of CRASH. Inheriting the facility made it an extension of the church, and we viewed its vast expanses of underutilized space as another physical plant to be used in service to people. We have no recollection that we ever discussed our feelings about or attitudes toward prostitution. What was relevant was that there was a particular need which we had the resources to meet.

Over the next months, we worked out the details of what would become the Professional Women's Clinic. Responsibility was divided up: We would care for the medical aspects, including education and training of staff to ensure that the treatment offered prostitutes would be no different than that other patients received; Jean would publicize the service among her former colleagues.

The target date for opening this new health service arrived, and passed, without one request for an appointment. Telephone calls to Jean went unanswered; she had vanished, leaving us in the lurch. We didn't know what to do and considered dropping the idea, but the tales we had heard of the exploitation of prostitutes had been too compelling. So instead we explored ways of making our own connections, and we decided to seek out the women where they worked.

In retrospect, what seemed like a catastrophe was really a blessing in disguise because we were forced to enter into and be educated about the life and world of prostitution *on their turf.* Assuming that we could establish relationships in a world so far removed from our own was surely the height of presumption, but our bullheadedness carried the day.

Thus, on a cold winter night in 1975, four anxious people met in a bar on Eighth Avenue. The cast of characters included Jane Hull and Pharis Harvey, in addition to the two of us. Jane, a former missionary, and Pharis, a Methodist minister, were longstanding members of Judson Church. Alcohol did not reduce our shared anxiety, and we tried to give encouragement to one another while laying out a plan of attack. The two women would walk slowly down Eighth Avenue, with Howard and Pharis following at a distance. When Jane and Arlene spotted women perceived to be prostitutes, they would approach and ask, "Are you a professional woman?" hoping the question would be inoffensive. An affirmative answer would be met with a thumbnail sketch of the medical services available and a printed card that listed the address, phone number, and hours of the Professional Women's Clinic.

Apprehensive but also curious, Arlene and Jane ventured forth, unwittingly dressed in the uniform of plainclothes police officers—slacks and pea jackets. As they started their walk down Eighth Avenue, scrutinizing each woman, their fear at first blocked the ability to determine who was and who wasn't. After a block or two they marshaled their courage and made several approaches. To their amazement, the women readily acknowledged that they were professional women but walked away before Jane and Arlene could begin their spiel. Lesson One: never disturb a working woman while she's trying to earn her living.

While we had failed to achieve our goal, the evening left us exhilarated. Arlene and Jane had overcome their fear, surmounting a personal barrier the magnitude of which would not be understood until later. Certainly we were all willing to try again, and over the following weeks the performance was repeated with greater discretion and sensitivity, but with the same disappointing results. The women were either too busy or too suspicious.

Frustrated and discouraged, we regrouped to consider our alternatives. Could we make contact more readily with women who worked in houses and massage parlors? Or should we admit failure and throw in the towel? Pessimism nearly carried the day, when someone suggested we purchase a copy of *Screw,* a weekly that carried a directory of all the massage parlors in Manhattan. This loathsome publication rated each of the parlors; its publisher had evidently sampled their wares. Graphically described were the facilities, some of the employees, and their areas of expertise.

With this information, Jane and Arlene plotted their itinerary, selecting several massage parlors within walking distance of each other. This stage of the adventure could not be shared with Pharis and Howard, but we would all meet later on. Anxious about facing another unknown, the women set out, list in hand. The first stop was Eros II, located just east of the main branch of the New York Public Library.

Arriving at the fourth-floor entrance, they encountered a

black man who was leaving. Registering surprise, he turned and followed them inside. Straight ahead, a young white man was seated at a desk. Sandwiched between the two strangers they felt vulnerable, fearing for their safety; they froze, unable to speak. After a few moments they worked up their courage and explained that they represented a new health service for prostitutes and wanted permission to talk with the women working there. The man at the desk didn't respond immediately. Perhaps trying to determine whether they were friends or foes, his eyes explored their faces. Then he smiled and, to their astonishment, said O.K.

For the next three hours Arlene and Jane sat in the parlor's reception area alongside customers and women. Both in a slight daze, they watched and listened to all that was going on around them. The population of the room changed constantly as new men arrived, those who were finished left, and the women drifted in and out. Although Jane and Arlene were old enough to be mothers to some of the working women, several customers mistook them for employees and chose them as their dates. The men were confused and embarrassed when told that the two visitors were not "working girls."

Engaging the women was surprisingly simple. They were friendly, interested, and unmistakably happy for the distraction of company. All but two of the fifteen women working that shift were white. Aside from the colorful body suits they wore, there was nothing distinctive about their appearance; they were just an ordinary group of young women. Their treatment of customers lacked artificiality or affectation, and they could easily have been working as salespeople at Macy's. Put at ease by their matter-of-factness and lack of self-consciousness, Arlene and Jane were able to discuss the services of the clinic and particular health problems several of them had.

In the mid-1970s, New York's massage parlors were relatively open houses of prostitution, most operating twenty-four hours a day. Women were employed on a week-to-week basis and usually worked twelve-hour shifts, spending most of their time sitting around waiting for customers to appear. They claimed that boredom was the least attractive aspect of their work, and many would knit or do crossword puzzles or read to pass the time. For a few months, paint-by-number sets were all the rage, and we wondered what customers thought when they walked into a parlor to discover a dozen artists in deep concentration. Prices charged for sexual services were set by management, which got a percentage, but women were free to negotiate for tips.

Customers were drawn to the parlors by advertising in papers like *Screw,* although many establishments would employ a "fly boy" who stood on the street nearby, handing out fliers to male passersby. These handouts would announce the existence of places like the Pleasure Seekers Club, the Taj Mahal, the Garden of Eden, Eros Leisure Spa, the Barbary Coast, the Velvet Touch, and dozens more. Invariably a woman in partial or complete undress was pictured; "complete satisfaction" was guaranteed, and the minimum price listed. On the West Side of Manhattan the range was between eight and thirteen dollars per session, while the East Side massage parlors commanded prices that began at ten dollars and often went higher than twenty-five. Price variations were not only due to the difference in real estate values; they reflected the racial mix of the women and the economic status of the customers. The least expensive parlors on the West Side always had a high percentage of black and Hispanic women employees and served mostly New Jersey commuters and minority males. Parlors on the East Side were lily white, with perhaps a token black woman, and they served what appeared to be a wealthier group of men. Decor ranged from grungy to elegant. The least attractive (West Side) were filled with furniture that looked as though it had been picked up on the streets. The most attractive (East Side) were planned with fantasy fulfillment in mind, and were plush and colorful. In one reception area, a caged mynah bird informed customers of the good time in store for them. A final East-West distinction was the color of management. On the West Side it was usually a black or Hispanic male; on the East Side, white men and women seemed to share the responsibility.

A customer would arrive at a parlor, choose one of the women from the reception area, and be led to a private room to undress. The woman would bring in a basin of warm soapy water to wash his genitals, at the same time examining them. From experience, she could usually detect symptoms of VD, in which case service would be refused. If a customer passed this test, negotiations would begin. Most sexual services had fixed prices (set by the parlors), but a woman would try to persuade the customer to buy the most expensive one; payment would be made in advance. There is no area of prostitution—the streets, parlors, houses, or call girls—where the fee is not paid up front. It is considered stupid, if not irresponsible, to trust a customer to pay afterward.

Arlene and Jane were stunned by the speed with which these sessions were concluded. In theory, customers were contracting for fifteen minutes of a woman's time, but they were usually finished in less than ten, and sometimes in five. The woman's goal was to turn her dates rapidly and return to the reception area in the hopes of being chosen by another trick.

Following the visit to Eros II, Jane and Arlene systematically visited every known massage parlor in Manhattan, and most of the experiences were good. Presenting themselves as representatives of both the clinic and PONY (a minor deception, since the organization was nonfunctional) facilitated far-ranging conversations. While the focus was on the services provided by the clinic and the health problems the women were facing, these often led to more personal discussions about their children, their men, their problems with management. It quickly became obvious that they welcomed the visits and asked that they be more frequent.

Visits were also made to some of the houses of prostitution the women would talk about. One evening Arlene and Eileen McNutt, a member of Judson, visited an apartment on the East Side that was devoted to meeting the needs of tricks who were interested only in S & M. The women, caught at a quiet time, were delighted to show the "church ladies" the tools of their trade: items made of leather and metal studs; ropes and chains, and various instruments for inflicting pain. The women were asked how they felt about their customers and the services they desired, and all were sympathetic to men who could only get their kicks through pain.

There were also times when Arlene and Jane were forcibly thrown out of parlors, usually on the East Side, but persistence sometimes paid off. In about six of the costliest and most elegant parlors, they never got beyond the receptionist. In one, they were able to get a bird's-eye view of the operation by "borrowing" a copy of the "menu" that was given each customer upon arrival. It listed the services offered: appetizers, main course, dessert, describing in detail the way in which the "food" was prepared.

Managements probably granted entry because they saw a way in which Jane and Arlene could be used. The parlors required that women have weekly medical examinations and get notes from the doctor stating they were free of venereal disease. In the event a customer complained that he had contracted VD after using the services of an employee, her doctor's note would be produced as proof that the infection had come from another source.

Management was unconcerned about the quality of the medical examination and testing. The women described some of the questionable practices: Doctors would test for VD by taking a smear, holding it up to the light, and giving the patient a clean bill of health; others did a cursory examination; and some gave notes in exchange for the fee. Everyone knew about these shortcuts, but management persisted in recommending doctors who should have been avoided. Dozens of women gave accounts of sexual services demanded by physicians, but because they needed the letter that was their license to work, they felt powerless to refuse.

The more we heard about the medical and personal abuse of prostitutes, the angrier we became. But our determination to make the clinic a viable alternative for as many women as possible was tempered by a need to adapt to certain realities, and out of that conviction was born the Monday Morning Clinic for Professional Women—Monday being the day the women traditionally went to the doctor for their letters. Facing us was the problem of providing documentation while adhering to the highest medical standards. Sound VD testing calls for cultures to be incubated for several days before a diagnosis is made, which means it is impossible to claim that anyone is free of VD on the day of her visit. Discussions with parlor managers confirmed that their interest was not in the authenticity of the testing, just the letter. To satisfy both the medical needs of the women and their obligation to employers, we devised a form letter stating that Patient X had been tested for A, B, and C and that the *physical* examination indicated no evidence of VD. Management found it satisfactory.

The Monday Morning Clinic never developed a large following. Perhaps twenty women became regular patients, and an equal number were erratic in their visits. To our surprise, *not one* had a positive GC culture, which was striking because in our regular gynecological clinic we had a high percentage of positives in a population that was young, white, and middle class. We had been told that almost all working women used rubbers with *every* customer, no matter what sexual act was performed, and their faith that it protects them against VD was borne out. Thus the myth about prostitutes as carriers of venereal disease was the first we were able to lay to rest.

Visits to massage parlors to spread the word about the clinic continued, and in time they turned into social occasions to which Jane and Arlene looked forward. The kind of intimacy that would come later through friendship with street women never developed inside, but the acquaintanceship fostered an appreciation of women who did highly unusual work. Occasionally Arlene and Jane would meet someone who worked both indoors and out, and from those women they came to understand the hypocrisy of a law that allowed the sale of sexual services in parlors but arrested and jailed for the same transaction entered into on the street.

Parlors on the West Side, particularly those on Eighth Avenue, operated in an informal way that permitted women to work on the streets if they chose, without being disqualified for future inside employment. There was more money to be made outside, where the range of potential customers was limited only by a woman's energy and her willingness to spend her shift walking back and forth between Forty-second and Fiftieth streets. But when the street got hot and a woman found herself getting picked up by the police with a frequency that hurt her income, she would spend the next few weeks working indoors.

On the East Side, this option was not available. If a woman was discovered working the streets, she could lose her job in the parlor or risk becoming unemployable in the future.

The 1976 Democratic National Convention was scheduled for New York City, and this provoked an outcry of alarm and concern that the existence of widespread street prostitution would impair the morals of visiting conventioneers. A more likely motive was that money spent impulsively for sexual services in Times Square would cut into the receipts of Broadway theaters, for which summer is often an arid time.

As demands to clean up Times Square increased, two "liberal" Manhattan legislators, Manfred Ohrenstein and Carl McCall, introduced a bill in Albany designed to grant the police broader powers for the arrest of prostitutes. One tool already at their disposal was the disorderly conduct law, under which women were picked up, taken to the local precinct, and more often than not released within a matter of hours. The other was the solicitation law, which required that a plainclothes police officer approach a woman suspected of prostitution and attempt to purchase sexual services. If a price was quoted, she could be arrested, and given a stiff fine or a jail sentence. Enforcement of the solicitation law was difficult and demanding because in no time at all the women passed along to their colleagues descriptions of the plainclothes cops, frustrating the quest for arrests. These efforts by the police were so routine that everyone expected them to be on the prowl, and as women arrived for work they would automatically ask, "Who's out tonight?"

The authorities wanted a mechanism that would enable them to make arrests efficiently, using the smallest number of officers yet achieving the maximum number of arrests. Protecting the rights of the women was an issue of minor importance in light of the determination to clean up the streets. The result was Penal Law 240.37, Loitering for the Purpose of Engaging in a Prostitution Offense. It empowered the police to arrest women observed repeatedly stopping or trying to stop people walking on the sidewalk or driving in cars; repeatedly having conversations with people walking by; repeatedly "beckoning" or waving to people walking by; or repeatedly interfering with people walking by. Such behavior was illegal if it was done for the purposes of prostitution, and therein lay the difficulty. How could a police officer determine the nature of a conversation being held a block away? Did she beckon to a man in order to ask the time? Did she engage in conversation with men she knew? Was she stopping people to ask for loose change?

Everyone banked on the complicity of the women themselves to make this new law work. Nothing in the history or experience of street prostitutes suggested they would protest an arrest—legal or illegal. The loitering law required no evidence that a crime had been committed, just the testimony of the arresting officer that one was *about to be* committed; thus the guilty pleas of the women would become the system's way of justifying each arrest.

While the debate over this bill was going on in Albany, Howard and Arlene met with a small group of people, including Margo St. James of COYOTE (Cut Out Your Old Tired Ethics), a California prostitutes' organization; the New York Civil Liberties Union; Marie Magoo of Scapegoat, a group formed to help prostitutes "escape" their pimps; and Henry Sturtevant, pastor of St. Clement's Church. Short of a constitutional test case, we felt powerless in light of mounting public support. However, through our contacts in massage parlors, we attempted to organize a letter-writing campaign; a handbill calling on working women to protect their livelihood was distributed by the thousands to parlors throughout Manhattan. Follow-up visits told us that few if any letters had been written, and the reasons were instructive. Not many of the women were registered voters; most lived in hotels and lacked a permanent residence. Those living in apartments did not want to be identified with the issue of prostitution. More important was their perception of being so far outside the system that protest in any form was not within the range of their experience. While we did not recognize it at the time, we were getting our first glimpse of the hierarchy within the world of prostitution. Those affected by the new law would be street workers, and they were held in contempt by their more protected peers, who believed that passage of the legislation would provide the others with their just desserts.

The lack of contact with women working the streets, who would become the targets of the loitering law, increased our frustration. Then, in June 1976, luck entered the picture and ended that isolation. Walking up Eighth Avenue to a meeting at St. Clement's Church, Arlene came face to face with someone she had encountered in various massage parlors. Stopping to chat, Patsy explained that with the onset of good weather, she had decided to work out of doors. She believed more money could be made on the streets and welcomed the increased freedom that came with being able to pick and choose her customers, stop in a store for a Coke, or take a coffee break. Later that day, back at the church, we decided we might have discovered the perfect opportunity for initiating contact on the street. Arlene returned the following day to the corner of Forty-fifth Street and Eighth Avenue, found Patsy at work, and asked if she could hang out with her. They had an especially good relationship—their sense of fun seemed to mesh—but in addition, Patsy, a gutsy woman, was willing to stick her neck out. She suggested that it was a crazy idea but in the same breath agreed to go along with it. Not everyone would have been able to take the guff she took from co-workers who couldn't understand why she would want an older, "square" woman around. That was a turning point in our work, and the beginning of a process of immersion that was to last through the winter of 1978.

During those first months, Arlene spent a couple of hours each day with Patsy, watching, listening, being introduced to other women, trying to take it all in, understanding some things, confused or bewildered by others, never asking a direct question for fear of seeming too curious, or being thought a voyeur or a reporter. Street people were told that Arlene's presence was to acquaint women with the services of the clinic —but the church connection was also known, and not particularly helpful.

Curiosity and suspicion greeted Arlene's daily arrival, and people would call Patsy aside to raise questions about the new addition to the street population. Interest was not limited to other women; pimps, tricks, street people, peddlers, cops, and everyone else who played a part in the street drama wanted to know what was going on. How Patsy interpreted the alien presence will never be known, but she seemed to satisfy her colleagues' interest, and some people would greet Arlene each day as she strolled from the subway to their hangout near Forty-fifth Street.

Quickly Arlene fell into a pattern of finding and standing with the same four women: Patsy, Joy, Pattie, and Coco. They were inseparable—except when one caught a "date"—and accepted her presence without comment. They would usually be found standing side by side in front of a hardware store. Wanting to be both unobtrusive and involved, Arlene placed herself directly behind them, close enough to catch most conversations, yet distant enough so that tricks would not approach her.

Interpreting these conversations was another matter, because the language of that subculture was new to Arlene, and efforts to understand without questioning made comprehension a slow and often tedious process. Commonly used words had other meanings; descriptive designations that were insulting and taboo in most circles were spoken with frequency and affection. For example, black and white women alike referred to their men as "niggers," and to themselves as "bitches." Unfamiliar with much of what was going on, Arlene concentrated on unlocking the mysterious nuances of those conversations. At the start—and unfortunately for only a short time—the events of the day were recorded in a log. The first entry poses the problem: "I arrived at about 12:30 P.M. and no sooner did I get there than Patsy whipped out a bunch of photos of her 'sweetheart.' I think 'my sweetheart' has a different meaning than 'my man.'"

Within a matter of weeks Arlene had gathered enough information to be able to follow most conversations, and when that happened, she relaxed a bit and became more attentive to the street environment.

There was a lot to observe. Women who work as prostitutes are very dependent on their senses for protection from those perceived to be the enemy: cops, tricks, other women's pimps, and crazies of all descriptions. In refining this skill, they develop a very particular way of seeing which enables them to absorb that which ordinary people might miss. Talking with a woman who appeared to be looking straight into her eyes, Arlene might discover that at one and the same time she was observing a police car turning the corner four blocks away on the left. Such highly developed peripheral vision is astonishing. It is also essential. One young woman spent many nights in jail until she finally had her eyes examined and got glasses to correct her myopia. After that she was arrested with about the same frequency as her co-workers. Prostitutes also have highly developed hearing, which enables them to screen out ordinary, nonthreatening sounds while it highlights those associated with distress or danger, such as the clackety-clack of high heels on the pavement, which tells them that unseen women are running from the police, or a passenger car screeching to a halt, suggesting that the cops are making a sweep arrest.

Intuition plays a major role in the way women interpret events and they rely heavily on it, especially when something is not absolutely clear or obvious. For example, if a woman spots a beat walker (cop), she will respond to that potential danger predictably by walking in the opposite direction. Yet on another occasion she may sense danger because of the way the street sounds, the way crowds are moving, the disappearance of particular people. Often, in the absence of a visible threat, senses and intuition still spell danger, and a woman will retreat to a coffee shop or a doorway. On nine out of ten such occasions, uniformed police, a squad car, or a gang of troublesome young boys will appear within moments. Such manifestations are extraordinary to witness.

Most of the time the women were open in discussing their customers, not unlike co-workers in any field. Patsy, who took some pride in her responsibility for Arlene's education, often shared what went through her mind as she selected dates. One day a very ordinary-looking man strolled past, and under her breath Patsy whispered that she didn't like his shoes. Arlene saw nothing unusual, but remained silent. When the man walked by again, Patsy repeated her comment, with greater emphasis. A moment later she disappeared from Arlene's side, and was seen entering a massage parlor with the guy whose shoes had disturbed her. Mystified, Arlene knew it was an occasion for breaking the rules and asking questions. When Patsy returned some fifteen or twenty minutes later, Arlene asked what had changed her mind about the man. Patsy's response was that the shoes initially made her suspect he was a cop, but when he came around the third time, she figured, given all the other women nearby, he could easily have made an arrest if that was what he wanted. Then with relish, and to demonstrate the accuracy of her intuition in these matters, she described what had happened inside the parlor. The customer had paid fifty dollars to cuddle against her and suck at her breasts while she performed a hand job, repeating over and over at his request, "You're a good boy, my son."

It would have been easy for Patsy to make the guy sound like a freak and ridicule him, but there was nothing in her telling of the story that suggested such a judgment. Rather, Arlene sensed her sympathy for a grown man who would need to get his gratification in such a way.

Throughout the summer of 1976, Arlene was sensitive to the widespread suspicion about her presence. Despite Patsy's mediation, many women wondered aloud about her motives for being there and her "real" attitude toward them and their work. Her silence and refusal to ask questions contributed to this uneasiness, although Arlene never hesitated to answer questions. The concerns that emerged most often were that she was there to "save" them on behalf of the church, or that she was a voyeur who wouldn't stay around very long. Aside from denying these accusations, there was little to be done except stick it out in the hope that time would show the women that they were wrong.

At the same time, the women tested Arlene in ways that were not always apparent. One hot and sticky afternoon, some of her acquaintances rejoined her after turning tricks, and began talking in unusually explicit terms about the blow jobs they had performed. Someone bought a bottle of soda pop and passed it around for all to share. When Arlene's turn came, four pairs of eyes were glued to her face, waiting and watching for any hesitation. As she took a sip, the women all smiled, and Arlene understood the nature of the test and that she had passed.

An opportunity to alleviate some of the suspicion arose when the New York Civil Liberties Union, of which Howard is a board member, agreed to publish *How Not to Get Hooked by the New Prostitution Law,* a handbook for prostitutes, their customers, and all people who might be arrested under the vague new law that was to take effect on July 11, 1976. Speculation about the law—how it would be enforced, what difference it would make in the lives of working women—was a constant subject of conversation. Because of our contact with prostitutes, we agreed to elicit the questions that best reflected these concerns, and NYCLU would provide the answers.

For several weeks, Howard would join Arlene on Eighth Avenue and park himself in a neighborhood coffeehouse. Arlene was to bring women over to express their uneasiness and misgivings about the loitering law, but things did not work out quite as we had hoped. Women would promise to come but would back out at the last minute. Others would end up sitting over a Coke tongue-tied, or staring at Arlene while talking to Howard. There were a number of reasons for this disappointing response. First—and perhaps most problematic for the women —was the fact that Howard is a minister. To them he represented a judgmental God who looked with displeasure and disfavor on their chosen work. No assurances from Arlene could change that. Second, in the life, the *only* men women talk to are tricks, cops, or their own pimp. That's a rule of the street, and we were asking them to break it, which at that point in our work and relationship they were unwilling to do. Despite this, sufficient input was obtained from the women, and our disappointment was tempered by a recognition that fear and mistrust of the square world would not disappear overnight.

When the pamphlet was published, early in July, we became the major distributor, and it was clear from the reaction that no one had ever really believed our story. That first day, a shopping bag full of pamphlets was toted up to Eighth Avenue, and they went like hotcakes. People, many of them unknown to us, came from all directions, wanting copies for themselves and their friends, and the repeated comment was "No one's ever done anything for us before."

Distribution was not limited to Eighth Avenue; over the next few weeks we saturated every area of Manhattan where prostitutes worked. Wherever we went—Lexington Avenue, Park Avenue, Third Avenue, Sixth Avenue—there was appreciation, and years later women would reminisce about the night we had come to give out "the books," and what a unique and important experience that had been for them.

How Not to Get Hooked was finally more symbolic than helpful; the vagueness of the new law prevented anyone from knowing with certainty how it would be enforced. The booklet's true value was in making clear to women in the profession the existence of two institutions concerned with their rights, NYCLU and Judson Church.

In the middle of August we made the transition to the nighttime world of prostitution. The majority of women worked evenings, and problems with the police occurred with greater frequency during that shift. Patsy worked only days, and, unwilling to arrive on Eighth Avenue without a friend to perform introductions, Arlene sought help elsewhere. Toya, who alternately worked days and nights, offered to act as a bridge, agreeing to meet her one Saturday evening at nine. Arlene was astonished by the number of women working—perhaps a hundred, none of them familiar.

Positioning herself toward the corner, some distance from the others, Arlene waited for Toya to appear. Time passed, but she continued to stand silently in the same spot. Finally a woman approached and said, "You'd better get out of here"; before Arlene could respond, she was gone. Moments later, another walked over and warned that Arlene should leave or risk getting hurt, possibly killed. That did it! The threat of violence caused her to freeze, and she remained helpless and terrified, unable to move to safety.

In the midst of her panic a woman came over, said she knew who Arlene was, and told her to ignore any threats because no one minded her hanging out. She was followed by another woman, who said much the same thing. It was a curious, confusing, and frightening introduction to the night life, but the transition had been made.

We met Big Kathy shortly after the transition from days to nights on the street. She was an exceptional businesswoman, who rarely stayed with a pimp for more than "a hot minute." With the money she made turning tricks, she had invested in a specialty shop in her hometown. It was run by her parents, while she took lengthy "business trips" to "buy new merchandise." Kathy was held in high regard by every woman we knew; they had great respect for her independence. For many, Kathy was an earth mother to whom the women could turn for advice and counsel. She always made herself available, and from what we heard, told it like it was. Kathy pulled no punches with her colleagues; at the same time, she understood that her way was not necessarily going to work for everyone.

Kathy took us under her wing because she immediately understood why we were there and wanted to play a part in educating us. Welcoming us warmly when we visited the parlor she managed and worked in, she introduced us to women we might otherwise not have met. Her help was invaluable, just as Patsy's had been earlier. Finally she retired and squared up, and we lost track of her. We heard that she had gotten married— to a cop!

For the next year, several nights a week would be spent on Eighth Avenue by members of the Judson congregation. Eileen McNutt, Jane Harvey, Gin Sligh, Marcy Doyle, Judith Thomas, Gloria Swinney, Mae Gautier, and many more joined Arlene on the street. They were people with a multitude of skills: A nurse would come along to discuss health matters with the women; a beautician would trim their hair; someone would help with housing and child care problems; and all of them, through their presence, let the women know that a congregation of people who made no judgment about their profession cared about them as human beings.

Once in a while a customer would approach and ask Arlene out. These incidents thrilled and infuriated the professionals, who would swear and shout, in voices which could be heard several blocks away, that the SOB had better leave her alone because she was a "Church Lady." How dare he assume she was working! He had better move on if he knew what was good for him! Troubled by a reaction that was counterproductive and that put distance between herself and the women, Arlene decided to handle such situations herself, and simply told the man she wasn't working. When women asked why she didn't deny being a prostitute, Arlene explained that doing so might imply she was better and different.

The women began to ask how Arlene could resist the financial temptation, and the discussions that followed helped her to understand more about them and their lives. A picture of the working women began to take shape; it was purely impressionistic, but nevertheless valid. White women often came from single-parent families where the father was absent and the mother an alcoholic. At a very early age they were molested or raped by a relative or family friend, and before their teens were institutionalized by the state or their parent for antisocial or criminal behavior. When they ran away or were released, with no salable skills or resources, they turned to prostitution for survival.

For minority women, the circumstances were different, and many had turned to prostitution because it afforded them economic opportunity generally denied by society. Their families tended to be more supportive, and the women remained in close contact with parents and siblings. It was the circumstances of their lives and the narrowness of choices open to them that propelled them into careers in prostitution, and the contrast between their childhood and her own helped Arlene to grow in understanding. Learning about herself through this exchange, she found her prejudices and preconceptions, her acceptance of the media-created mythology about prostitution and prostitutes, being eroded by firsthand experience. Though she had considered herself free of prejudice in the beginning, it was only when she acknowledged with surprise that the women were in most ways not dissimilar to girls she had known in her lower-middle-class Bronx high school that Arlene realized her unconscious expectation that they would be. While a few of the women had been to college, most were comparable in intelligence and awareness of the world as young file clerks might be. They enjoyed rock concerts, soap operas, and pretty clothes, and their conversations were not unlike those you could hear on any subway during rush hour.

The most common myth, the one that says that prostitutes are junkies, was quickly laid to rest. An expectation of heavy drug use was not borne out; instead the reality was that the women smoked marijuana (and in recent years have indulged in occasional cocaine use) but shared a contempt for heroin addicts. Some, like Mona and Ebony, fit the stereotypes, but they were the exceptions. Other women avoided and criticized them for using prostitution to support their habit, and Arlene was often warned to have nothing to do with them. Ignoring this advice, in the years that followed we became very involved with Mona.

A multi-drug abuser (heroin and alcohol), Mona taught us about those prostitutes who use drugs to ease the pain of their lives. Until the age of eleven, Mona lived in upstate New York with her mother; her father had abandoned them during her infancy. Mona remembers her mother as a woman who drank a lot, but who was not an alcoholic. Occasional male friends would visit their home. When Mona was nine or ten, one of them abused her sexually. She tried to tell her mother about the incident, but was not believed. Unable to find any comfort at home, Mona began spending an increasing amount of time on the streets. This did not seem to trouble her mother, but neighbors were concerned and reported the situation to the Bureau of Child Welfare. After their investigation, Mona was removed from her mother's home and placed in foster care.

She remembers the family she lived with, and their two young children, with great affection. They made her feel as though she belonged. About a year later, her mother died in an accident, and Mona's only thought was that she would never have to go back. Life with her foster family continued pleasantly enough. She did well in school and made friends in her new neighborhood. When she was twelve, her foster mother was diagnosed as being terminally ill. Mona wanted to remain with the family through this time, but the Bureau of Child Welfare felt it an inappropriate environment. She was removed and placed in a state institution. Miserable, lonely, and afraid, Mona ran away, winding up on the streets of Buffalo with no money and no skills. That first night, she slept out on the streets. The second day, at the age of thirteen, she turned her first trick.

When we met Mona she was in her early twenties. Bright, remarkably sweet, but at the same time a sad young woman, she was helplessly addicted. Eventually she sought our help to enter a detoxification program. After three weeks at a local hospital, she was released, with no place to go and no money to support herself. We tried to help for a while, but she couldn't bear being dependent. She had applied for welfare, but the slowness of the process was discouraging. Finally she just gave up and went back out on the streets.

Over the next few years, Mona would appear at the church with some regularity to ask for our help to enter a hospital for detoxification. We never refused. From time to time she would stay at Arlene's apartment for a few days, as members of the congregation nursed her around the clock until she was well enough to make it to the hospital.

Mona thought she needed drugs to ease the loneliness. Her

man, himself a junkie and drug dealer, was in and out of jail. Usually she would try to clean up her habit when he was away. When she was drug-free, she would reminisce about the foster family she had lived with and their two young children. It was clear that she longed to have a child of her own, but no matter how hard she tried, she was unable to conceive.

For several years, we watched Mona get on and off the drug merry-go-round. We had no real hope that she would ever kick her habit and make a life that brought some happiness. But in 1982 she became pregnant. When she learned that a child was on the way, she reentered the hospital and finally succeeded in breaking her addiction. During the pregnancy she would occasionally stop by the church and sit around spinning out her plans for the child. Her pallor was gone, her hair glowed, and the fingernails she had always bitten were long and shapely. During this time, Mona was broke and living in shelters for the homeless. Despite this, she stayed away from the streets and her former companions.

Mona's daughter was born, healthy and not addicted. The last time we saw Mona, she was buying books on child rearing in a Village bookstore. She has since left New York City, and is leading a square life in another part of the state.

It was harder to ascertain the falsehood of the myth that women are forced into prostitution by evil and manipulative pimps. While there are certainly cases where this happens, the truth is that most women freely—and here it's important to bear in mind limited opportunities—choose to enter the profession.

Part of the difficulty was that we brought to the subject of pimps deeply ingrained prejudices which prevented us from hearing and seeing anything that conflicted with what we already believed. It took a full year of going back and forth on the issue. One day we would think that maybe pimps weren't *all* so bad. But then the prejudice would take over and whatever had caused us to doubt our earlier conviction was forgotten.

Probably what made it so hard to think that perhaps pimps weren't all bastards was the feeling that no one would believe us. But then we came across a slim paperback book entitled *The Politics of Prostitution,* published by the National Organization of Women in Seattle. It was based on research by Jennifer James, associate professor in the Department of Psychiatry and Behavioral Science at the University of Washington. James is one of the few scholars who have done extensive research in the field of prostitution, and on the issue of pimps (as on other matters in the life) she confirmed our impressions. Unfortunately, the book is out of print, but for us it became a bible. Whenever we wondered whether our observations were crazy, off the wall, unbelievable, we would check James, only to discover that she saw and heard the same things.

Where pimps are concerned, especially their role in coercing women into prostitution, James's research bears out what women have told us—namely, that their entry into the profession was not at the behest of some man looking to make a buck off a woman's body. In fact, it is the circumstances of women's lives and the narrowness of choices open to them, not some all-powerful pimp, that motivates them. Once in the life, many choose to be with a man society labels a pimp because, like the rest of us, prostitutes need someone to love and be loved by, and pimps are the only men they know who do not judge and reject them because of their profession.

Another popular myth concerns the pimp as the source of all violence directed at prostitutes. Some do beat their women, but probably as many square women are injured and abused by husbands as prostitutes are by pimps. (Some of the most important conversations we had centered on just this issue. In talking about violence, women would preface their remarks with the phrase "In this life . . ." indicating that women outside the profession were not physically mistreated by their men. We always took advantage of those occasions to raise the larger issue faced by all kinds of women, not just prostitutes, in the hope that they would see themselves, in that respect at least, as not altogether different from their square sisters.)

Most serious injuries are inflicted by "tricks." The illegality of prostitution encourages some men to view the women as easy targets, worthless and degraded human beings about whom society is unconcerned. And of course they are right! When beaten, no matter how badly, a woman is unlikely to report the incident to the police, who are perceived as adversaries more than protectors. Over the years, we've taken many women to emergency rooms with injuries suffered at the hands of customers. Guns, knives, metal pipes, and baseball bats are often the weapons, but in some parts of Manhattan it's the automobile. A young woman we knew was run over and killed at her workplace, and afterward the driver reportedly got out of his car, turned to his companion, and said, "Imagine going to jail for killing a whore." In the years we have been out on the streets, many women we knew were killed, but not one of their deaths was at the hands of a pimp.

In the late 1970s, there was an unlimited amount of money to be made on Eighth Avenue. It was not uncommon for a woman to end an evening with five hundred or six hundred dollars in hand; the sky was the limit. Because money was so plentiful, the massage parlors where women brought their dates usually had an empty orange juice jar or milk container into which they would toss loose change or dollar bills, which were considered more a burden than an asset.

One evening, as Arlene was starting her routine walk down Eighth Avenue, women stopped and urged her to go to Big Lou's massage parlor, saying he had something for her. She had no idea what they were talking about, but hurried along to Forty-fifth Street. Inside, a dozen women were sitting around taking a break, and a very angry and unhappy-looking Big Lou was standing in the doorway. He pointed to the money jar that rested on the floor. When it had been filled to the top, the women had decided to make a donation to Under 21, a program for runaway youth operated by Father Bruce Ritter just across the street, and Big Lou had taken the contribution over earlier that day. Several hours later the jar was returned with a message that Father Ritter refused to accept "dirty money." Everyone had been shocked and hurt. Believing in the work Ritter was doing to keep runaways off the streets, they had wanted to help.

It is hard to believe that Ritter could have been so contemptuous of their act of generosity and goodwill. After the money had been returned, the women caucused and decided to make the donation to Judson Church. Big Lou handed Arlene the jar, and she had less than a moment to decide whether to accept it or not. Her ambivalence stemmed from the days of illegal abortions, when we had been offered kickbacks by abortionists who hoped to bribe us into sending more patients. We always refused, but joked about all the churches we could have built.

The offer of the money jar brought back those memories, but the pain the women felt over Ritter's rejection of their humanity was visible, and Arlene could not bring herself to do anything more than accept with thanks. Relief passed over the faces in that room, and Judson's Sunday offering that week had an extra $148.

3

Learning to Stand in Another Woman's Shoes

> The streets are cold
> Growing old each passing hour
> But the cold
> Has frozen an ice age inside.
> There is no fuel
> To melt the frost
> It's been consumed already.
> The nights
> Endless and lost
> Without permission
> To scream out
> The loneliness.
> Silent betrayals taking
> Form in the mind
> Only to return
> A touch
> Without touching.
> Beginning and ending
> A hollow dream—
> A hollow dream.
> —DIANE

By the end of 1977 we were accepted fixtures on Eighth Avenue, although a few women refused to have anything to do with us. (One of them made a nasty public fuss whenever Arlene appeared. This woman just couldn't understand why anyone in her right mind would choose to be out on the street on a cold and snowy night when she could be comfortably at home watching television.) Most were friendly, and some intimacy had developed. On occasion, women turned to us in illness or times of trouble, and we had taken some to the hospital with injuries suffered at the hands of tricks, and sometimes their pimps. They also turned to us on more joyful occasions: Howard Moody had baptized several of their children, and some of the women held a baby shower for a co-worker in the church garden one summer afternoon. We also provided more mundane but no less essential services. One of the more unusual was in response to a phone call from Lisa, who needed help replacing two hundred dollars in charred bills. She had stashed the money in the lower part of her oven and forgotten about it. Then, the night before, Lisa had broiled fish for dinner and remembered too late about the money she had hidden. Afraid to take the burned bills to a bank and risk having questions asked, she wondered if we could help. Coincidentally there had been a small fire in the church office several weeks earlier, so we took her money to our bank, explaining that it had been burned in the fire. The manager replaced it without any questions and Lisa went happily home.

On the whole, we felt comfortable and protected, and all fear of the street had vanished. We had begun discussions with some of the women about our idea of publishing a newspaper directed toward and distributed to working prostitutes. Remembering the reception given to the NYCLU pamphlet, we thought such a publication could be informative and also make more visible the concern felt by some people in the square world.

The women's response was cautious. They showed no real enthusiasm for the idea. One told us it would be like "casting pearls before swine." She believed most of her colleagues were too selfish, stupid, and ignorant to appreciate such a venture. However, others, like herself, would find it valuable and she wondered whether there was a way to distribute it selectively.

We decided to go ahead, and with the collaboration of some

women, named the publication *The Hooker's Hookup: A Professional Journal*. The Statement of Purpose said, in part, that "every profession has its magazine, every trade its journal, so why not those women who sell recreational sex. . . . We hope that it might serve the needs and speak to the issues that concern women on the streets." We printed a thousand copies of the first issue and distributed them without cost; they were gone within a couple of weeks. The women were delighted and proud to have a publication that was "theirs." We learned later that some copies had been "given" to police officers, or taken from women who were arrested. In subsequent years, women who didn't know each other would strike up friendships in jail when one saw another reading the *Hookup*. It was a sign that she was probably in touch with the "church people."

The first issues of this "occasional journal" were pretty thin, containing reprints of articles we thought the women might find interesting. However, by the third issue we had hit on several devices that enriched the *Hookup* and made it truly "theirs." First we introduced a column called "Telling It Like It Is," in which a question about their lives would be posed. For example, in one issue it was "What do you like best about your work as a prostitute and what do you dislike most about your profession?" We printed the question on forms with plenty of room for answers and distributed them to anyone who was interested. Over several weeks, women would write their responses and return them to us for inclusion in the next issue of the *Hookup*. We never edited their writing; freedom of speech ruled the day.

Secondly, we included a section of poetry and prose, which the women offered to us voluntarily and with considerable pride. It surprised us to discover how many poets there were and how rich and wonderful some of their work was.

These innovations thrilled the women, who were proud to see their work and names in print. Of course, some who wanted to make contributions were afraid to use their names, and would instead sign their work "Anonymous," "Unknown," "Me," etc. As each issue appeared, women would try to guess who the author was, and it became a game in which most everyone would participate.

We had also gotten to know the shopkeepers, and were on friendly terms. Those relationships grew out of the Con Ed blackout of 1977, on an evening when Gin Sligh and Arlene were out on the street. They were visiting at the Sugar Shack, a small parlor on Forty-seventh Street, when the city went dark. The doors were immediately locked and everyone was warned against going outside, where it could be dangerous. Women feared that looters would arrive and strip the shops while police were engaged elsewhere, but after an hour Gin and Arlene grew impatient and insisted on leaving. In Gin's car, parked nearby, they talked about what they should do and could do to help. It didn't take long to figure out. Racing to the church, they came back with hundreds of brand-new brightly colored candles. Along Eighth Avenue, they handed them out to everyone —shopkeepers, women, and street people. There was probably no greater service they could have provided under those circumstances. As they left Eighth Avenue there were tiny pockets of light where women stood, candles in hand, trying to catch dates on those dark streets.

That evening we earned credit with the shopkeepers, who had locked their safety gates but remained inside stores and restaurants to ward off thieves. For weeks afterward, they would express both appreciation and surprise that we had shared our largess of candles with them, and friendships were cemented.

Even the police had come to know and accept our presence. Women told us of their curiosity, for which we were thankful. We had realized from the start that one of the Judson women might accidentally be arrested by an officer who mistook her for a working woman. Howard had explained our presence at the local precinct, but there remained a possibility that word had not reached the beat walkers and plainclothes officers. With the passage of time, and frequent reports of police interest from the women, we became complacent, and our fear of arrest receded. We were wrong.

On the evening of January 7, 1978, Arlene headed uptown for a quick visit. A special celebration was to be held at Judson early the following morning, but an invitation by a twenty-four-year-old woman named Little Bit had to be honored. Little Bit had been toothless most of her adult life. Understandably self-conscious about her appearance, she had been saving every penny to buy false teeth. That evening, heading straight to the street where Little Bit worked, Arlene found her with a full set of uppers and lowers. Complimented and asked how she felt, Little Bit smiled painfully and said, "They're killing me!" With that she burst into laughter and removed the plates.

Arlene was headed toward the subway to go home, when someone stopped her to say that Beth was ill and looking for her. Beth was one of the women we had come to know best and with whom we spent a great deal of time. She was respected by everyone: younger women came to her for advice and counsel; older women looked to her for comfort. A role model for many, she even had the respect of some pimps. After twelve years on the streets, there was not much she had not experienced, little she didn't understand, and she had become Arlene's mentor, the person she turned to for explanations. Beth never asked anything in return and Arlene understood the limits of their relationship.

Months earlier, Arlene had been surprised to discover that Beth did not see herself as the terrific person we thought she was. When one of her colleagues had been assaulted by a passerby, Beth had intervened, fought off the man, and comforted the woman. Afterward, Arlene casually mentioned how nice it was for her to help when no one else would. No sooner were the words spoken than Beth turned and, in a tight, shrill voice, said she was definitely not a nice person and not to make the mistake of thinking otherwise.

The news that Beth was ill caused Arlene to change her plans.

She had never asked us for anything, so she had to be in a bad way. Arlene found her outside a bar-restaurant on Forty-sixth Street, in a group of twenty other women, with such painful stomach cramps that she couldn't stand upright. They were waiting for her man to come pick her up, but he had not arrived. Arlene agreed to wait around until midnight, and then, if Donald was still not there, take her to the emergency room at Roosevelt Hospital.

During that time Arlene talked with the women who moved back and forth between the street and a hallway. Shortly before midnight they were clustered together in front of the restaurant. Arlene was engaged in conversation with Lisa when the group was approached and surrounded by three young white males dressed in jeans and jersey pullovers. One knelt on the sidewalk, eyes bright, gold earring glistening in the reflected street light, arms outstretched, and said, "Now what you're going to do is walk single file across Eighth Avenue. And if anyone moves out of line or makes a break for it or does *anything,* I'll crack their head open." Silently the women fell into line, and Arlene followed, afraid to speak or in any way attract attention to herself. It was not until everyone was in unmarked police cars that she realized who the men were. They had neither identified themselves as officers of the law, told the women their rights, nor said why they were being arrested.

As they were taken inside the Eighteenth Precinct, women mumbled under their breath that the cops were going to be furious when they realized they had made a mistake in arresting Arlene. It was hard for her to know what to do; she was terrified, fearing that the police would harm her or the others. At the same time it was clear that everyone was in the same boat: picked up in an illegal sweep arrest. There was no way to disassociate herself; they were all innocent! So Arlene remained silent as they were led through the precinct and placed inside a large barred holding pen.

After whispered conversations about Arlene's predicament,

it was agreed that it would be best for everyone if she kept silent until she could make a phone call. That strategy had the advantage of alerting someone outside the precinct to the fact that she was in police custody, which would inhibit police retaliation. Also, that person could come to the station, explain the officers' mistake, and have her released.

While waiting, some women napped on the floor, some on the few benches, and others sat facing the wall, covertly putting colorless nail polish on their fingertips or burning them with matches in the belief it would change the configuration of their fingerprints.

In the meantime, their arresting officers decided to go back out on the street to make more arrests, in order to fill what they said was their quota for the night. Almost two hours later they returned, disappointed. They had not gotten as many women as they wanted; people had been frightened off the street.

Finally the women were taken to the booking desk for fingerprinting. The officer asked names, addresses, and ages. Finding it difficult to get a clear set of Arlene's prints, the officer asked what she had done to her hands. Without thinking, she told him she did a lot of needlepoint. She hoped he would ask about employment, and so resolve the issue, but he didn't.

Afterward, permitted to make a phone call, Arlene reached Howard, told him of the arrest, and asked him to come and get her out. When she returned to the holding pen, everyone began to speculate on how long it would take for Howard to get to the precinct and how soon Arlene would be released. Time passed, and one by one the women were taken to be strip-searched, but Arlene's name was not called. Then a woman who had been searched returned to tell of overhearing a conversation between two officers. Howard had arrived at the station, but the police thought he was a fraud and had refused to let Arlene go. No one could believe it, and the women kept up their vigil until Arlene's name was called and she was led away to be searched. Images of the degradation caused by a stranger's intimate examination of one's body ran through her head as she was taken to a room where several officers were seated at desks. One of them offered her a cigarette, and heartened by that act of generosity, she asked whether she might refuse to be strip-searched. The response was that of course she might refuse, but they would "crack her skull and break her head open and conduct the search anyway."

Moments later a matron arrived. Leading Arlene into the adjoining bathroom, she had her undress, squat, and bend over, as she explored her body for hidden contraband. Later we learned that women arrested for prostitution (a misdemeanor) are routinely strip-searched, while only those males arrested for crimes of violence (felonies) are accorded the same treatment.

From the search she was returned to the holding pen and from there taken to a cell and "bedded down for the night." Her cell was perhaps four feet by six and contained a wooden bench (no mattress, no blanket, no pillows) on which to sleep. Also in the cell were a miniature toilet (but no toilet paper) and a doll-size sink (lacking soap or towel). It was almost five o'clock in the morning, and Arlene leaned against the bars feeling suffocated by the loss of freedom and wondering what the hell was going to happen.

No one could sleep that night. Women in various parts of the cell block screamed all night, and no effort was made to silence them. Not that it would have made a difference. The bench was unyielding, and it was cold; Arlene's short pea jacket was insufficient cover.

The following morning at eight o'clock the matron walked through the cell block instructing all prisoners to be ready to move. Cells were unlocked, and everyone was marched downstairs, where a paddy wagon waited to take them to court for arraignment. There must have been thirty women, and as they checked names off on a list, each had her left hand placed in a handcuff which was attached to a long heavy chain. In groups of six they were packed into the wagon, most standing because there were too few seats.

They arrived at 100 Centre Street—the Criminal Court—in less than fifteen minutes, and were taken through a maze of hallways to a holding pen. Before entering it, they were again strip-searched, this time in full view of male officers walking by.

Time passed. Women slept on their coats, putting a little distance between their bodies and the cold, damp concrete floors. Lunch was served: spoiled bologna sandwiches and tepid tea, which most women discarded. Fights broke out, and several women were removed to another cell. In the center of the cell, the open toilet, which afforded no privacy, backed up and the odor was overpowering. Their arresting officers came by several times and claimed that the reason for the delay was that some fingerprints had not yet been returned from Albany. The implication was that no one could be arraigned until all prints had cleared, which was a falsehood.

During the ten hours spent in that cell, the women took care of Arlene, and she had cigarettes long after her own had run out. Mindy insisted that Arlene nap on her fur coat. Others started complaining to the matron that Arlene didn't belong there and had been falsely arrested, but the matron ignored them.

Finally, at 6 P.M., the arresting officers returned to take them back uptown for the night; they would not go to court that day. In the hall, as they were being put back in the chains, one officer stated that it was Arlene's prints that were causing all the trouble. By that time, upset and angry, she told him it wasn't true. She was certain he knew that he'd made a mistake, but he didn't answer.

The ride up to the Fourteenth Precinct, on Thirty-fifth Street, was a nightmare. Whatever route those officers took, there were bodies flying all over the back of the wagon. Those women who were standing were jolted from side to side, falling over one another. It was deliberately vicious and vindictive.

At the precinct house they were again taken to be bedded down in spartan cells, after yet another strip search by the matron. What contraband the women might have in their possession after two prior searches and twenty hours in police custody was not specified; it was standard operating procedure.

Exhausted and depressed, Arlene lay down on the wooden bench and fell asleep instantly, only to be awakened by the matron, who told her she was wanted downstairs. She was taken to the commanding officer, whose desk was just off the main lobby, and through the bars could see Howard Moody and Paul Chevigney, a volunteer lawyer for the New York Civil Liberties Union. They had obtained a writ of habeas corpus, and Arlene was released into their custody.

The following morning we all met with an assistant district attorney, who, while hostile and unfriendly, dropped all charges. A month later NYCLU filed a lawsuit against the police and all public officials involved, charging false arrest and false imprisonment. At the same time a class-action suit was filed in federal court, seeking to have the loitering law, under which all twelve women had been arrested, declared unconstitutional.

The arrest and the subsequent lawsuit solidified our relationships with the women and laid to rest any remaining suspicions or doubts about who we were or why we were there. It was an event with which all the women could identify; even the pimps had come to recognize that we were not merely do-gooders out to convert the women. At the same time, we had come to understand in a very intimate way that the exploitation and oppression of prostitutes comes largely from society's laws, which criminalize, harass, prosecute, and punish only the woman involved in the act of selling sex. What mattered most about Arlene's arrest was that it was not significantly different from the everyday experience of women in the profession.

By 1978, we had witnessed dozens of illegal arrests. The first of these was in a coffee shop on Eighth Avenue where Arlene was having dinner with three working women. As dessert arrived, a police officer entered, approached their table, pointed to the three women, and said, "You, you, and you. Get your coats on. You're going to jail." The women complied, leaving Arlene with four pieces of apple pie and an understanding of their powerlessness.

The lesson learned that evening and reinforced over the years is that prostitutes are only rarely arrested for committing a criminal act. They are almost always arrested because of who they are, where they happen to be, and what they do for a living. The police know them by sight and usually by name, and feel free to arrest them with impunity whenever they choose. It is not uncommon for a woman to be picked up by the police as she steps out of the cab that brought her to work, or on her way to the market for food, or as she dines in a restaurant.

And this sometimes continues long after women have left the life. Last year we ran into Ming in arraignment court. She had "squared up" in 1979, had married, and was living in New Jersey. Nevertheless she had been arrested for loitering as she walked by the New York Hilton; the officer remembered her from the old days. She was furious, but because she had a lengthy arrest record she pleaded guilty to the charge.

This criminalization forces the women to lead unstable and continuously disrupted lives. Without proof of "legitimate" employment, they are unable to rent apartments, and live instead in costly hotel rooms, spending between a thousand and fifteen hundred dollars a month in some run-down place that is willing to rent rooms to prostitutes. And then, when they are arrested and spend a couple of days in jail, they are unable to pay their rent, which is due on a daily basis. (Places that rent to prostitutes often refuse to give them special monthly rates, which might be offered to other customers.) Then management plugs the lock on their room and takes all their belongings in lieu of payment. Deirdre once said that prostitutes are "society's greatest consumers" because they buy the same things over and over again.

The majority of prostitutes are mothers, and this is almost always the result of planned parenthood. Women choose to become pregnant by the man they are involved with; if they have the slightest suspicion that a pregnancy resulted from turning a trick, they will usually have an abortion. The memory of a trick's broken condom around the time of conception is usually enough evidence for a woman to terminate a pregnancy.

Always at the mercy of the police, women never know when they set off to work whether the day will end in jail. So most of their children are cared for by twenty-four-hour baby-sitters in apartments scattered throughout Manhattan. Many of these sitters are themselves former prostitutes or the mothers of prostitutes. One of the sitters we know, who takes care of perhaps five children at a time, is a loving and concerned woman. Twice when children were left for extended periods by their mother, with no money paid for their upkeep, she continued to provide care at her own expense. Mrs. W. becomes very attached to these children and often has difficulty giving them up when their mothers' lives change or they move to another city. Two of her own children had been prostitutes and they were her connection with colleagues in need of a baby-sitting service.

Other women send their children to their man's family to be cared for. This is particularly true of white women who have maintained little or no contact with their parents. Because they usually bear interracial children, they find greater acceptance in the black community, which is also more tolerant of the work they do. Yet due to these living arrangements, a child is with its mother only on her day off, so both are denied any opportunity for a normal relationship. Only when we understand how important children are to these women can we appreciate how poignant the separation is.

We had some reason to believe that Arlene's civil suit against the city would make manifest the reality of prostitutes' day-to-day existence. While we had no expectations of winning the constitutional test case, it was important to challenge that law. If we had let the arrest pass, people (the women in particular) could have drawn any conclusion they chose. But a lawsuit was a public statement of our opposition to the status quo and put us solidly on the side of the women in their struggle with the authorities.

There was a lot of press coverage, probably because not many forty-two-year-old Jewish employees of the Protestant Church get arrested for prostitution. The media were a little puzzled when they discovered that we were not out proselytizing the women, and they didn't quite know how to deal with the work we were doing. As a result, the coverage for the most part was neutral.

The night after a press conference at NYCLU, we went to Eighth Avenue to check out the women's reaction to media reports. As we emerged from the subway at Forty-third Street, people called and shouted that what we were doing was wonderful and they wished us luck. It was astonishing how many strangers stopped to offer good wishes. While the women were delighted with our attempt to get the system to pay for its mistake, they were also critical of Arlene's demeanor on television. Some thought she looked as though she was about to cry.

It was a celebratory night on Eighth Avenue. People talked of little else and there was an air of excitement about the future. It was also the beginning of a mythology that would build around the event. Even today, older women will share with younger ones the details (often highly exaggerated) of how the police mistakenly arrested Arlene and how they finally paid after she sued them in court. Beth, who escaped arrest that night, continues to brag about her role in the event.

The progress of the lawsuit was slow and boring. But finally, three years after it was filed, we went to trial in federal district court. It began with the civil suit, a jury trial to determine whether the police were guilty of false arrest and false imprisonment. While not a circus, the trial did have drama. To begin with, everyone was in costume: the judge in his robes, Howard in his clericals, the police in their polyester suits, and Arlene in demure dresses and suits borrowed from women of the congregation. We had not been lucky in drawing Federal Judge Thomas P. Griesa, who with his Mormon background brought a set of clear prejudices to the situation.

The trial for false arrest and imprisonment took less than a week. The jury was mixed in age, race, and sex and the NYCLU lawyers thought we had a good chance of winning. While we expected the police officers to lie, we had not expected them to doctor the arrest records. These, when presented in court, placed Arlene and the women arrested with her in locations different from the arrest site. The greatest problem the police faced was having to disprove our allegation that there had been a sweep arrest. So they testified that on the night in question, they had observed Arlene for some time engaging in conversation with men who they assumed were tricks. They even recalled the men's races and ages, though the location of the supposed encounters was a block away from where the arrest occurred.

Prior to the trial, Arlene had been asked by the NYCLU attorneys to meet with a sympathetic psychiatrist, who would testify at the trial. Along with Howard and Arlene, he was the only other witness for our side. While our lawyers would have liked it to be otherwise, Arlene was unwilling to ask the women arrested with her that night to testify. There were a number of reasons for her resistance. On the one hand, it could have been interpreted as self-serving, and have affected relationships with the women, who might have felt compelled to do something they would probably have preferred to refuse. On the other hand, like the women themselves, we doubted they would be believed, and we feared the police would retaliate if they testified. In fact, one woman volunteered to testify and was subsequently threatened by the police. Some months before the trial, she was approached by an officer who asked if she was Ginger. When she admitted that she was, he told her that she must be mistaken, because Ginger was dead. She interpreted this encounter as a threat against her life, designed to discourage her from being a witness at the trial.

After a week of testimony, the case went to the jury, which deliberated two days before bringing in a verdict of not guilty on the charge of false arrest and guilty on the charge of false imprisonment. It was a blow and a disappointment, but $7,500 was awarded for false imprisonment. The constitutional case was yet to be heard, but we were pessimistic about its outcome.

In preparation for the oral arguments, Judge Griesa decided to educate himself about the issue of prostitution. He decided to go out on the street to observe the situation himself. Arrangements were made, and on a Friday evening a black limousine containing the judge, his driver, two members of the police force, the lawyer for the district attorney's office, Arlene, and Richard Emery of NYCLU went out. It resembled a guided tour, with the police providing the running narrative as they drove up Eighth Avenue and down Ninth. The evening ended abruptly when the car stopped for a light in an area where transvestite prostitutes work. One approached, stuck his head in the limo, and asked Judge Griesa, who was in the front seat, whether he'd like to have a good time. If body language speaks, the judge was shocked to his shiny black shoes. He rolled the window up and announced that the tour was over.

What Griesa saw and learned that night was probably not very helpful to the constitutional case. If there was any open-mindedness at all, the transvestite's solicitation closed that door. After hearing the arguments and considering the amicus brief submitted by the Legal Aid Society, Griesa issued his opinion, denying our petition on the grounds that:

> The statute is not unconstitutionally vague, since it describes in definite terms both the proscribed conduct and the criminal state of mind—*i.e.*, repeatedly beckoning, stopping, interfering with, engaging in conversation, etc. people in public places, for the purpose of engaging in or promoting prostitution.

Nor is the statute overly broad in the sense of impinging on lawful activities. The evidence in the case, including the observations of the Court, confirms the well-recognized fact that there is a great amount of prostitution solicitation activity which is clearly identifiable as such, and which is easily distinguished by the police from lawful conduct.

While we had lost both cases, we were greatly relieved to have the whole business behind us. We were naturally disappointed, but less so than NYCLU, which had expected to win the case. With a little effort, they persuaded us to appeal both decisions, a process that took several more months but produced the same results. The only path left open at that stage was the U.S. Supreme Court. NYCLU was willing to consider such an appeal, but we were opposed and persuaded them that it was best to let the matter lie. We believed that the circumstances of the case, particularly the apparent self-interest (that is, our involvement in working with prostitutes), made it a weak case with which to test the loitering law. If we had taken the case to the Supreme Court and lost it, other challenges, perhaps stronger and with a better chance of success, could be denied a hearing at that level.

From the point of view of women on the street, the suit for false arrest and false imprisonment was perceived as having greater importance than the constitutional case. Certainly they could more easily identify with a challenge to the police that claimed false arrest, since they themselves were often falsely arrested. They were sorry and shocked when the jury found for the police on that part of the case, but they were delighted when $7,500 was awarded for false imprisonment. It was as though our making the system pay for its mistake vindicated all women who were subjected to erroneous arrests.

We interpreted the women's lack of interest in the constitutional case as evidence of low self-esteem. There was no way in which they could envision a time when the law and law enforcers would not be pursuing them. Explaining what might happen if we won on the constitutional suit was like telling a fairy tale. Women who work as street prostitutes have no hope that they will ever be treated differently, and suggestions to the contrary are simply beyond their comprehension and experience.

At about the time the lawsuit was resolved, we began feeling a need to broaden the base of our contacts in other areas of Manhattan. We also wanted to create an environment that would enable us to get to know the women in a more intimate and private way. We thought about renting a storefront on Eighth Avenue, but could not afford to take that step. We also realized that going that route would be a mistake. Over the years we had been out on the street, we'd watched as the women shifted their base of operations from Forty-fourth Street to Forty-sixth Street to Forty-third Street, from west to east, usually in reaction to police pressure. If we had opened a storefront on Forty-third Street and the women found themselves working on Forty-eighth, we were certain that they would not venture away from their workplaces, especially if the police had caused them to move to new locations. And women who worked in other parts of Manhattan would have neither the time nor the desire to travel to Eighth Avenue, no matter how attractive a space we created. All things considered, a fixed location was clearly the wrong way to go.

In the mid-1970s, Judson had faced the same dilemma in attempting to serve the health needs of disaffected youth on the Lower East Side, and had resolved that problem by purchasing what came to be known as the Judson Mobile Health Unit. The unit became the model for us in our desire to provide prostitutes with a private place for them to gather, away from the prying eyes of the men in their lives—pimps, tricks, police. For some months we looked at mobile homes, but we discovered that they were either prohibitively expensive or poorly designed. Frustration grew until one day we noticed the small buses used by car rental agencies to transport airline passengers to and from the airport. We knew this vehicle would suit our needs. The seating was informal, arranged like a horseshoe, with an open space in the center. So we negotiated the purchase of a 1978 Chevrolet van for what seemed like a reasonable price.

Purchase of the bus was financed by our denominational parents, the American Baptist Churches of Metropolitan New York and the Board of Homeland Ministries of the United Church of Christ. Over the years, both had helped finance projects Judson was involved with, although the ministry to prostitutes was probably the least understood and most controversial work we had undertaken.

We wanted to create an environment that made the women feel they were in a living room, not a bus. So Essie Borden and Michèle Edwards of the Judson congregation reupholstered the seats and made curtains to cover the windows; Lee Guilliatt furnished two miniature paintings; and the narrowest coffee table imaginable was made to fit in the center of the bus.

The first night we took the bus to Eighth Avenue, the women told us of several additional things they would like. The first, and most important, was a bulletin board where they could display photographs of their children for other women to see. In the life, women rarely carry things of value in their purses because there is always a possibility that they will be robbed by a trick, or a street person. So family photos were rarely brought to work for fear they would be lost. A bulletin board on the bus would be a safe way of displaying them. We quickly had one installed above the driver's seat, and within weeks it was covered with snapshots of the most beautiful babies one could hope to see.

Until that happened, we were unaware of just how baby-oriented women who work as prostitutes are. They take pride and pleasure in their own children and the children of their co-workers. While most of those we have known were mothers, the ones without children were no less interested. Often they were involved and served as aunts and godmothers. Mothers would exchange old photos on the board for more recent ones, and often they would sit around trying to guess the parentage of an infant whose photo they had not seen before. But there was always a poignancy to the "baby board" because some pictures were reminders of friends who had moved, squared up, or died. Sometimes with pleasure and other times with sadness, the women would discuss what the children were doing, or looked like, years after their mothers were no longer out on the street.

Another early addition was a sign posted at the entrance to the bus. We had to make it unmistakably clear in the beginning that the bus was not to be used as a sanctuary by the women when the police were chasing them. Still, we didn't know how to phrase what needed to be said directly but inoffensively. The women on Eighth Avenue solved the problem for us and put it in the following way: "Welcome! If you're running, run right by; if you're walking, walk right in." Our church secretary, Leslie Dennis, a calligrapher, made an attractive sign which could not be missed by any woman coming on board. That made it unnecessary for us to badger each new woman who came inside; others would point it out and interpret its meaning.

The sign was particularly important because in preparation for the bus, Howard had met with police department officials, explaining our intentions and seeking their cooperation. As a result of Arlene's lawsuit, we thought they might be suspicious of our purposes and consider them confrontational. While they were not, we wanted an understanding that could prevent trouble with the police before it began. The official Howard met with, and the department, were cooperative, and in March of 1980 a training memorandum went out to precincts in Manhattan describing the bus and its purpose. It stated that "it is the avowed intention of the project's sponsor to avoid providing sanctuary or a working headquarters for prostitutes . . . it is entirely probable that some prostitutes will take advantage of the situation to further their own ends. If such a situation is observed the police officer should make this known to his commanding officer so that the project operators can be contacted and given an opportunity to take corrective action." The final and most important words were: "Invasion of this vehicle or harassment of its occupants will not be tolerated."

Through the years there have been instances where ignorant, rookie cops harassed the bus, particularly when it moved into new locations. After reading the memo, which we always kept on board, they would apologize and leave us alone. But not once did the police "invade" the bus and attempt to make arrests, although it sometimes must have been a thorn in their side to have to wait until the women chose to return to work.

With the help of the Eighth Avenue women, we set some informal rules which were adhered to wherever the bus traveled. First, no men (aside from Howard) were permitted on board. This excluded tricks, pimps, and cops. The second rule was that there could be no alcohol on the bus unless we brought it (which we did on special occasions: eggnog at Christmas and champagne at New Year's). The final rule was that the women might roll joints (marijuana) on the bus, but if they lit one, Arlene would smoke it. Since they couldn't imagine such a thing, she was never put to the test.

Because it was a "church" bus, some of the women felt uncomfortable talking as they would on the street, but we encouraged them not to worry about language. That would have made the environment unnatural, and the women as well as ourselves uncomfortable. Despite our relaxed attitude, there was hardly a new woman on the bus who didn't apologize the first time she used a profanity, and only after others assured her that it was O.K. would she relax.

The first night the bus went out, we were armed with hot chocolate, chicken broth, tea, and homemade cookies provided by members of the Judson congregation. But we were very uneasy about our reception. We had spoken to women in the Times Square area about our intentions, and they had been encouraging. However, in their world promises are rarely fulfilled, so we thought it possible that their assurances were based on the assumption that the mobile unit would never become a reality. We needn't have worried. When we arrived at Eighth Avenue the women were lined up and waiting. Everyone came on board to inspect and comment; some stayed for a while to chat, others asked for a hot drink and went back to work. We were clear in our minds that if the bus was truly to "belong" to the women, they, not we, would need to set the agenda each night. That meant conversation would center around whatever their concerns were at the moment.

One question dominated the first months of the mobile unit's life, and we heard it repeated over and over from many of the women who came on board. They wanted to know what else the church used the bus for. Didn't we use it to transport kids to Sunday school or to take the elderly on outings? As we heard that concern raised time and again, we realized that what they were communicating was their disbelief that something was being done just for them. Some of the women asked the question more than once, despite our negative answer. While we had considered using the bus for other church needs, as we began to understand how important it was to the women that it belonged to them, we decided against other uses. This was all underscored one day when a call came from a woman who works in Times Square, asking what the bus was doing parked on Third Avenue during the day. She had seen it while passing by in a cab and was upset because it disputed our claims about its use for other purposes. She was reassured when we explained that the bus was at the repair shop and, too large to be brought inside, was parked on the street while the mechanic did his work. However, the message came through loud and clear.

One reason we wanted to have a place for women to gather

was to make contact with those who worked in areas of the city other than Times Square. We were curious about whether our observations in that commercial district were unusual, particularly where the police were concerned, or whether prostitutes everywhere in the city shared a common experience. The second place where we attempted to make connections was on Lexington Avenue in the Twenties. Large numbers of women, almost exclusively black, worked there late in the evening. So we drove over and parked the bus about half a block from the hotel where they sometimes took their tricks, and sat and waited. In the midst of the group of women Arlene recognized one she had known on Eighth Avenue. So she went over to greet her and explain what we were doing there. As she returned to tell Howard that Little Debby had been receptive and that perhaps the next time we were there the women would come on board, Little Debby was leading the women toward the bus. The incident was subsequently duplicated in other parts of the city, where our arrival would be eased by the presence of someone we knew from Times Square who could act as our interpreter and assure her colleagues that we were O.K.

During the next few years we became particularly close to the women working on Lexington Avenue, sharing with them especially the loss of murdered friends. One of the many people we became particularly fond of was Bonnie. She would come on board the moment the bus reached Lexington Avenue and leave only when we got ready to depart. Bonnie spoke with a deep Southern twang, and the other women adored her sense of humor, her talent as a mimic, and the genuine goodwill she had toward all her colleagues. She would always sit in the same spot on the bus and keep everyone laughing as she described some trick she had been with the night before, or a street experience she considered bizarre. Often she would talk about her family. Her father ran a gas station in a small Georgia town, and while Bonnie was fond of her parents, she became rebellious when her father insisted that she have nothing to do with black folks. To her mind he was an unreasonable bigot. She liked the blacks she knew in school. As a teenager Bonnie found a way to get back at her dad. Each day after school she spent several hours pumping gas. When blacks would drive into the station she would fill their tanks and take their money, and as they started to drive away, she would toss the bills they had given her back into the car. Before long her father caught on and she was banished from the station, but by then she had made friends among the young black men and would sneak out to spend time with them. By the time she graduated from high school she'd been involved in several relationships; she decided to go where she could date any man she liked without being criticized. She came to New York and she met Jimmy. They decided that together they could make enough money to assure a happy future: Jimmy through the sale of drugs and Bonnie through the sale of sexual services. They shared a comfortable apartment in Queens and in the years that we knew her, Bonnie never appeared less than happy in that relationship.

She arrived at work each evening wearing an ordinary knee-length dress, and sat on the bus drinking hot chocolate and sampling the sweets. Over time, a ritual developed around the departure of the bus. As we were getting ready to leave Lexington Avenue for our next stop, Bonnie would rise from her seat, remove the belt from her dress, gather and lift the skirt until the hem was a dozen inches above her knees, replace the belt to keep the newly created minidress in place, say goodbye, and go to work. This was done without any self-consciousness on her part and after a while we hardly noticed as she redesigned her evening's outfit.

Bonnie was murdered in the fall of 1980, and the shock and grief of the loss we shared with her colleagues was immeasurable. For months afterward, the bus was a place of mourning. It was as though her absence left a void which no one quite knew how to fill, and with her co-workers we would reminisce about the things she had said and done. Invariably someone would start a conversation with, "Remember when Bonnie . . ." and for the remainder of our visit, stories both old and new would be told, shared, and embellished. Finally someone suggested that we create a permanent memorial on the bus. We got a photograph of Bonnie, which we framed, and from then on it sat prominently on the serving table. Later it would be joined by photos of other women who died, but for a year Bonnie's picture stood alone.

Bonnie was one of the only white women working in that particular area, which made the reactions to her death more striking. The women who mourned her were largely black and Hispanic. In other parts of Manhattan, we knew, minority women often felt resentment toward whites because they usually made more money; however, none of it was directed toward Bonnie, in life or in death. This made us wonder about the reasons for our own acceptance. After all, we were white people, representing a white church, yet we never felt any hostility directed at us because of our race. Probably we could have been Martians and still been accepted by women who were simply appreciative of any interest and concern from the square world.

Prostitution on Lexington Avenue is different from the sale of sexual services on Eighth Avenue. In Times Square, with its heavy foot traffic, women choose their tricks from men walking by, ignoring catcalls and queries from johns in passing cars. All dates are turned in hotel rooms within a block or two of where the women work. But on Lexington Avenue, most customers are in cars, which women approach as they stop for traffic lights. Often these men don't want to be bothered with parking their cars or the cost of a hotel room, and so they are known as car tricks. Women negotiate the service and the price before entering the car and driving off to a deserted street in the area. If these women had their druthers, they would turn all tricks in the comparative safety of a hotel room. But often it's a choice between getting in a car with a stranger or not making any money, so women take the risk. Sometimes, a colleague will jot down the license number, make, and model of the car a woman has driven off in, so that if she doesn't return within a reasonable length of time, that information can be given to the police. (We know of no instances in which this has happened.)

One of the safety rules of the street is that a woman should never get into a car with more than one man. It's considered foolish and dangerous to be outnumbered in a moving vehicle. Occasionally, when money is tight, women will take the risk anyway, believing that their safety is secondary to their stash. One night, Mickey drove off with five young guys who hired her to work at a midtown bachelor party. When the church bus arrived, she had been gone for more than two hours and her "wife-in-law" was anxiously awaiting her return, while at the same time criticizing her "stupidity." Their man always warned against taking such chances, but Mickey had not "broken luck" and was feeling desperate. A precaution she had taken was to insist on partial payment in advance, and she had given the money to her wife-in-law for safekeeping. In the event something happened, at least they would have her two hundred dollars!

From time to time there were discussions on the bus about the merits of working in an area where car tricks were the norm and hotel tricks the exception. While there was no argument about the safety issue, it finally came down to the fact that like most people, women who work as prostitutes are resistant to change. That which is unknown or foreign is frightening; that which is familiar is safe and comforting. The Lexington Avenue women worried about being hurt or killed, but despite that concern were unwilling to shift their base of operations. Even stories like the one Simone told about being kidnapped by a trick and driven to Queens, while the driver held her hostage with a gun, were not sufficiently alarming. Although Simone had escaped when the car stalled at a red light, there were others who were not so lucky. Other discouraging tales circulated through their street network about women who had died because some crazy trick "went off on them," but the stories had little effect. At first it was hard to understand how the women could be so fatalistic about their profession. But as the years went by and we heard of and knew about women who had been murdered in hotels and cars, on deserted streets, in subway stations, and in their own beds, we realized that it was the profession that was dangerous, not necessarily where or how one worked at it—danger is a by-product of the illegality of prostitution. A group of "lawbreakers" held in contempt by society are perceived by deranged men as worthless women and natural targets for their aggression.

Within weeks after meeting the Lexington Avenue women, we began taking the bus to Delancey Street, another area where street prostitution flourishes. We had been warned against this by some women on Eighth Avenue, who believed that anyone working there would be tough, hostile, and unappreciative, if not downright contemptuous of our presence. Nevertheless we went ahead after discovering that some women we knew spent time on Delancey Street, which gave us a natural entrée.

Preparing for our first visit, we steeled ourselves for a radically different group of women. What we found instead was a group of women who were probably less well educated than their sisters on Lexington or Eighth Avenue, but nevertheless as pleasant and friendly as women working elsewhere in Manhattan. They stood in darkness, along a thoroughfare where all the shops were closed and gated, trying to solicit car tricks. Police cars passed frequently; on some nights the officers moved the women or arrested them, while on other nights they ignored them.

It was there that we heard some of the grimmest stories about police harassment, a very different problem from illegal arrests. On the Fourth of July that year, we arrived on Delancey Street shortly after the police had driven by, throwing ash cans at the women. We were horrified at the image of defenders of the law lifting garbage cans and tossing them at people. Looking around, we couldn't see a single can on the street, and doubted the women's truthfulness until they explained that ash cans are giant firecrackers. The squad car had passed by several times and the officers had tossed the lighted and illegal objects into the women's midst, then had driven away laughing. We were enraged, but the women, accustomed to harassment by the police, were only moderately angered.

The casual telling of these stories astonished us. Abuse by the police was accepted as part of the price to be paid for working. Dishonest, corrupt, disturbed individuals getting their kicks by harassing and arresting helpless women—such police were on a par with the women as persistent lawbreakers. This observation was reinforced time and again in different areas of Manhattan, within different police precincts. On Eleventh Avenue, men in squad cars would force women to give up their wigs; in winter, police would take away their shoes; sometimes they would corner the women in a one-block area, give them fifteen minutes to catch a date, and arrest all those who failed.

We quickly developed a regular visiting pattern for our evenings on the street. We would leave Judson at about 10 P.M. and head for Eighth Avenue, which remained our favorite location because our work had started there and we had developed some of the most intimate relationships with that group of women. It is the area where police activity and frequency of arrests are the most intense. Our involvement began in the days when massage parlors were thriving and money was plentiful, but we had seen the area change as the Mayor's Task Force, claiming moral outrage but appearing to act in the interest of real estate speculators, gradually closed them all down. By 1984, most of the women working on those streets had been forced to move to other locations around Manhattan, both commercial and residential.

As long as women we knew continued working there, we

drove first to Eighth Avenue, spending an hour or two parked on the corner of Forty-fourth Street. Depending on how much money they had made before we arrived, some women would stop in just to say hello, others would sit and chat. When things were tough and the cops were giving them a hard time, the bus would fill to capacity as they waited for a change in shifts. (Tours of duty for the police are normally 8 A.M.–4 P.M.; 4 P.M.–midnight; midnight–8 A.M.) Occasionally the police would park their squad car alongside the bus and glare, frustrated by their inability to make arrests while the women were safely on board.

On Eighth Avenue, the bus drew the interest of passersby. Often, when curiosity got the better of them, people (usually men) would press against the windows and try to peek in. Or they knocked on the driver's window, asking questions. Most of the time the women would take care of these meddlers, but on a couple of occasions when interest from the street was running unusually high, they decided that the best way to get rid of snoopers was by raising their voices in song. So for five or ten minutes the bus would be filled with sounds of a revival meeting, as the women sang hymns with energy and gusto. It always amused them to think that they had put one over on the public by creating the impression that they were being "saved."

Not that the women make fun of religion. On the contrary, most were raised in the church, and while they may no longer attend services, they retain a loyalty and identification with the traditions of their youth. It was not hard to discover who was Catholic, because whenever those women needed to see a doctor or enter a hospital, they chose St. Clare's or St. Vincent's (both of which are operated by the Catholic Diocese). Many considered the bus a church, and women could often be heard shouting to their friends that they were "going on the church" for a while.

Several times on Eleventh Avenue, as the women were getting ready to leave the bus, one of them, the daughter of a fundamentalist preacher from Nevada, decided to lead us all in

prayer. Everyone stood holding hands as she asked God to protect them from the police and see to it that all the johns had
plenty of money to spend. The prayer was delivered with so-
lemnity, as were the Amens that followed.

On Lexington Avenue, after the murder of a co-worker, the
women asked Howard to lead them in prayer as they sat on the
bus, and later requested that he perform a memorial service for
their friend at Judson.

Howard is the primary driver of the bus and Arlene is almost
always on board. When Howard is out of town, members of the
Judson congregation, both male and female, do the driving.
Once in a while, women from the congregation have come
along as visitors. So long as we explain that they're from our
church, their presence never inhibits conversations. It is a reflection of the women's trust that we have been able to bring
strangers on board without affecting the environment.

At times the presence of a new face has triggered conversations that might not otherwise have taken place, like the one
about bigotry. From the beginning we realized that some of the
women shared certain prejudices. For example, there was an
attitude toward Jews which could have been interpreted as
anti-Semitism. As a Jew, Arlene found this painful, but was
afraid it would impede the work to confront it head-on.

In the publicity surrounding Arlene's arrest and lawsuit,
some newspaper articles which mentioned that she is Jewish
were reprinted and distributed on the street. The women,
many of whom had never known a Jew aside from some of their
tricks, were astonished. This confusing new fact modified but
did not eliminate their prejudice.

We also became aware of a prejudice toward black tricks. It
was based on the belief that black men always wanted more
than they were willing to pay for, and caused many women
(both black and white) to refuse them as customers. Pimps,
themselves usually black, were the source of this attitude and
often instructed their women not to turn black tricks, possibly

out of fear their women would be stolen from them.

The women's attitudes toward homosexuality reflect the anxiety of their men regarding lesbian relationships. Often when women leave the life they go through a period in which they reject any contact with men, and pimps may traditionally have interpreted that as a tendency toward lesbianism. Nothing in our experience supports such a conclusion, but pimps are not immune to developing a mythology that protects their interests.

An opportunity to deal with this arose the night a gay member of our church drove the bus. As we were parked on Lexington Avenue, several women called attention to a "faggot" who passed by, and made fun of him. After a while they became interested in Bill, a young and attractive man in his early thirties, and Meechie asked how old he was, commenting that he was cute and probably married. Arlene held her breath, concerned about Bill's feelings and wondering how he would respond. Hesitating only a moment, Bill told the women that he wasn't married, he was gay. They were stunned by his admission and apologized for anything they might have said that hurt his feelings. The incident turned into an open discussion about homosexuality, in which the women acknowledged that gays were a minority, like themselves, oppressed by society for their sexuality, and on that score there were more similarities than differences.

There were contradictions in these prejudices, however. The few working women we encountered who were Jewish were fully accepted by their peers. Their faith was not a barrier in relationships with their co-workers. On Eleventh Avenue, a transvestite male worked easily among the women; his sexuality posed no problems. In discussions on the bus, he participated fully and the women treated him like an equal.

In 1982, we asked the women's consent to cut back on the number of nights the bus was out on the streets so that we could spend additional time in court. Very reluctantly they agreed.

Our presence and the comforts of the bus would be missed. But we explained that we needed a fuller understanding of how their lives were affected by the judicial process. We had always been open with them about the ultimate goal of our work: to eliminate all laws that made prostitutes criminals. The next step in our education was knowledge of the courts. We had seen how the police enforced the law on the streets; now we needed to observe how the courts and the judges responded to this enforcement.

4

The Prostitute Through
the Eyes of Others

A girl never needs to go hungry
She just starves all her life
The nourishment that she seeks
Is hidden in some strangers eyes
She knows she is missing something
But can't figure out why
And she can count on her fingers
All the times she let it slip by
It sifted through her fingers
But left residues in her heart
But she never needs to worry
Or to fret or to feel lonely
Because a girl never needs to go hungry
Only empty in her own eyes.

—KIMBERLY

All of us know how important are the attitudes and perceptions
of others in the process of identity formation. What others think
about us, how they see us and treat us, is—in part, at least—how
we form our self-identity. This is as true for "the working
woman" as for anyone reading this book. When we are the
recipients of admiration, caring, and especially love, we tend to
build strong self-esteem. Without these gifts, life is much more
difficult and a strong knowledge of who we are is highly improbable. One would think, then, that streetwalking prostitutes—
who experience the hostility of the populace, isolation by parents and friends, and a regular pummeling by the media—
would be dysfunctional basket cases; yet most of them are not.

And since many are hard-working survivors of a dangerous and debilitating occupation, we have to assume that they are seen and treated in a variety of ways within the social context of their working lives. We of Judson know from our experience with prostitutes that the most important ingredient in what we had to offer was our respect for them as human beings and as women engaged in a difficult occupation. How do other men and women perceive prostitutes, and the effect of that occupation upon their lives?

Our first insights came from the group of Judson women who, in the very beginning of our work on Eighth Avenue, were involved in helping to establish relationships. Indicating they were neutral about prostitution and without any ax to grind, they were willing to let themselves be informed by experience. Listen to some excerpts from their journal, a record kept for only a brief period during the spring and summer of 1976:

Tiny and I were standing together when a guy came up to talk to her. I moved away. They talked and he said something to her about "policewoman"; she shrugged him aside and walked slowly up the street. The guy stood about five feet from me and watched me for a while and then left. Tiny came back and, after considering it, I asked if the guy was uncomfortable about me—I was a little paranoid. She said no; she just didn't want to go with him. I then said that if we were causing anyone any trouble, she and the other women should let us know because that was not what we were out there for.

Sometime later I walked over to where they were. Joy said to me, "Look, we appreciate what you're trying to do but it's not gonna work. You don't even look like prostitutes—I mean you're all older. Oh, I don't mean any offense, but you must be thirty or so, aren't you? I mean, those cops know us and they're not going to take any chances on arresting anyone but us. So I don't think what you're trying to do is gonna work."

She told me she'd just finished a year in training school. Said she's been in and out of those all her life. She pulled out of her purse a small photo album and showed me pictures of her family. There were four or five brothers and sisters. She said they all have different fathers. One sister looked all black, one brother all white, and her mother is white with some Indian blood.

At this point we were together, and a sailor came up to Cookie and began to talk to her, but she had bad vibes and moved away. A rather large black woman went up to him and began talking. The sailor said he had a hotel room and asked her to bring along another girl for his cousin. Cookie said, "That's not true; those guys live on their ships." But either the black girl didn't hear, or she didn't care, since she went off with him. They walked up Eighth Avenue and Cookie said to us, "That sailor's a cop." We followed them and sure enough, on the corner of Forty-sixth Street there were two plainclothesmen waiting. The sailor took the black woman up to them and they took her off to jail!

We talked about photographers and they mentioned that they really don't like to be photographed for television because they all have families and people whom they don't want to know what they do. Sandy kept saying it was embarrassing. Her family had already seen her on television once or twice, she thinks, and they don't believe her when she denies it is her.

A woman named Tammy was quite upset about the law and kept asking rather desperately what they could do. She was exhausted from having been up for a long period of time and had been drinking a lot and was looking for much more in the way of reassurance than we were able to give her. She made me very uncomfortable at one point when she chewed out other women in the parlor for not paying enough attention to us and giving us the "respect" due to persons who were trying to "help" them. I was worried that this would result in her alienating the others from us, but they seemed to take it in their stride.

I asked Karen if she knew any of the Judson women. She said no, but probably because she was out mostly at night—midnight on. I said we didn't go out that late because the street was rough and we were not used to it yet. She agreed it was probably good that we stuck to days and evenings. She asked me why we were out. I told her that it was because of the new law which will affect all of us and we are trying to get to know the women and let them get to know us. She seemed really pleased with this answer.

Back on the street we talked at length with a woman named Honey, who seemed glad of our being there and was very warm and open. She told us some real horror stories of some of the violence that has occurred to herself and other women. She has a bad scar and still suffers nerve damage from a trick's assault.

It was not long after Arlene and others from Judson began hanging out on Eighth Avenue, standing alongside the women as they worked, that they got a heavy dose of how some other "square" women view female prostitutes. At around 10:30 or 11:00 P.M., as theaters let out, couples walking down the street toward subways or parking garages would pass by groups of working women trying to catch dates. The male's face was usually expressionless, but his female companion would glare at the women, her face reflecting a variety of emotions: contempt, rage, disgust, embarrassment, annoyance. No effort was made to mask their feelings; it seemed as though they deliberately made eye contact to ensure that their message was received. And the message, as Arlene and others perceived it, was primarily one of anger.

Such women communicated silently, but there were others who were not content with this chancy exchange. They were the ones who tried the tolerance of working prostitutes by verbalizing their feelings. A nasty comment would be directed at the women, something like: "How disgusting" or "Dirty bitch." Remarks like those really ticked the women off and were rarely allowed to pass. They would elicit from the prostitutes verbal retorts intended to cause embarrassment. They were cleverly done; they not only called attention to the woman but made her feel insecure about her relationship with her male companion. Responses would be something like: "Where do you think he goes after he takes you home?" or "Hey, bitch, you're no better than me. At least I don't give it away!" Women working as prostitutes never sought out these confrontations, but neither did they back away when they felt a square woman had gone too far.

One evening, as Arlene stood with a group of prostitutes, several couples passed by, the women's faces filled with an anger impossible to miss. Afterward, when the crowds thinned and the street was quiet, Arlene asked the prostitutes how they felt when that sort of thing happened. Weren't they furious (as she was) that anyone would assume a superiority? Didn't they want to shout and scream that no one had any business behaving as though the working women were worthless pieces of dirt? They smiled almost indulgently at Arlene, and trying to soothe her ruffled feelings, told her that after a while, like themselves, she would get so used to it that she wouldn't even notice when a square woman exhibited "an attitude."

Those random street experiences were especially upsetting because in the nature of their work prostitutes rarely come in contact with any segment of society that is exclusively female. Unlike the men they know, who are either tricks, cops, judges, or pimps, the women they deal with are usually individuals operating on their own or in some large, institutional setting. Working prostitutes extrapolate from those encounters and sometimes assume that all square women must be their enemy.

If we were to speculate about the hostility some square women express toward prostitutes, we would have to say that they feel threatened by the existence of women who treat their sexuality so casually that they are able to engage in sex for money. In a society where women are at the threshold of equality with men, beginning not only to enjoy sex but also to decide when and with whom to have it, the prostitute becomes the embodiment of that freedom which until now has been only a fantasy.

Many prostitutes understand this: not because they have immersed themselves in the teachings of the feminist movement, but rather out of the experience of their own lives. One evening at the Judson-sponsored Professional Women's Clinic, a patient asked Arlene and Jane if they had ever fantasized about being prostitutes. The moment the question was posed, they knew they had, and wondered how many other women had permitted their minds to toy with that possibility. Could it be that fantasies about prostitution are as common as those about rape?

Pimps also believe that square women are envious of the sexual freedom prostitutes exhibit for the world to see. Arlene was confronted in the early days with the accusation that she was really "getting off" by hanging out on the streets as the women turned their tricks. This was perhaps carrying it a step too far, but the point being made was that there had to be some envy and/or identification with what the women did when they took their dates into the massage parlors. Certainly there was a fair amount of curiosity.

Not all encounters street prostitutes have with square women are unpleasant. There are women like Sister Betty, a middle-aged black who, in the late 1970s, when massage parlors flourished on Eighth Avenue, pulled her shopping cart from Forty-second to Forty-eighth Street, stopping in each parlor to chat with the women. She would ask if anyone was hungry, and if so, would reel off the contents of the dinners packaged in insulated trays that were stacked in her cart. Usually there would be chicken or chopped steak, along with a green or yellow vegetable and something like macaroni and cheese. The dinners were carefully wrapped and still steaming when they were opened; the servings were generous and the price was right: two dollars a meal. Sister Betty clearly liked the women and treated them with respect. Once in a while she delivered a short lecture on nutrition, and she never left a parlor without blessing everyone who was working there.

The service she provided was valuable, since most of the time the women ate at fast-food restaurants, or settled for junk food. Sister Betty provided an alternative that was nutritious, inexpensive, easily available, and tasty to boot. Women who worked on the streets (but turned their dates in the parlors) would often follow as she walked up Eighth Avenue and into a parlor, where they would buy a dinner and eat it on the spot.

Sister Betty told us she was the deacon of an evangelical church that was located in a building in the Times Square area, and that providing meals to women working as prostitutes was her ministry. Indeed it was! Unfortunately, when the parlors disappeared as the city cracked down and closed them in the early 1980s, Sister Betty vanished as well.

At around the same time, we had an experience that taught us a lot about the variety of attitudes square women have toward prostitutes. A young woman stopped by the church office to inquire about our street work. She presented herself as a student at a New York university, writing a paper on prostitution and looking for information that would be helpful. There was an edge to her voice and her manner was initially hostile, but after an hour of conversation she admitted that she had been in the life and had worked on Eighth Avenue for some six years. After squaring up, with financial assistance from her family, she lived in SoHo and was a nursing student. Expressing surprise that we made no judgment about the profession, she continued to drop by once in a while to chat. We learned that since the time she had left Eighth Avenue Crystal had been totally alone. She had given up friendships with her former colleagues but had not developed new ones with square women. Afraid that they would look down on her for her past, she had chosen to keep it secret rather than risk rejection.

Judson became increasingly important to her because it was the only place where her former profession was not only known but considered irrelevant, and it provided a sense of security absent elsewhere in her life. An excellent student, she anticipated graduating from the nursing school with honors. But as graduation neared, Crystal became aware that the process of applying for a license to practice nursing was going to force her to make a critical decision. One of the questions on the application dealt with arrests, and of course Crystal had been arrested repeatedly during the years she worked on the streets. For weeks on end we held intense discussions about whether or not she should answer that question truthfully. Crystal finally decided that the short-term benefits of lying (that is, getting her nursing license) were far outweighed by the risk of having the truth emerge at a later time in her career. So she admitted to having an arrest record, and in accordance with the policies and procedures of the New York State Department of Education, she was denied a license.

Crystal was, and is, one gutsy woman. She refused to accept that decision lying down. No question of competence was involved in the decision to deny her a license; after all, she had graduated second in her class. She made the decision to challenge the bureaucracy and hired a lawyer to represent her. Before she could proceed, however, she needed to be certain that she could count on the support of the dean of the nursing school and her adviser. In order to win that support she had to confide her past employment to both women. She says it was the hardest thing she ever had to do. During her student days, the dean and her adviser often let her know how impressed they were with her work and her commitment. She feared they would be terribly disappointed when they learned the truth. She was wrong, and much to her amazement, they were not only sympathetic but also supportive. Both agreed to testify on her behalf at a Department of Education hearing at which the decision to deny her license was to be reconsidered.

We also testified on Crystal's behalf, and after several months of deliberation the department reversed itself and granted her a license. She presently heads the intensive care unit at a major hospital. While the future seems promising, she lives every day with the fear that her past will somehow catch up with her.

Crystal had not expected that the staff of the nursing school would be unruffled by the discovery that one of their best students had been a prostitute. She mistakenly assumed that their attitude toward her would be adversely affected. When that didn't happen, she decided to reconsider her unwillingness to share her past with other women. Maybe not all of them would put her down. In the years since, she's formed close friendships with several women, each of whom knows that she once worked as a prostitute.

For some women things turn out differently. April, a tall, strikingly beautiful woman in her late twenties, was just beginning to think about leaving the life. Fortunately, her mother, with whom she was very close, knew what she did for a living but still wanted her to come home to New England. About a year after we met, April made her break with the streets and moved back to the small town where she had been born. From time to time we would receive letters from her asking about former colleagues and keeping us informed of the progress she was making in her new life. Having, with her mother's help, found a clerical job in a training program, she sounded as if she was doing well, and mentioned that she had been dating a man who worked in the same office. We were delighted that things seemed to be working out for her.

Then one night, about six months after she left New York, we spotted April standing in front of the little grocery store on the corner of Forty-fourth Street. Arlene left the bus and went over to speak with her. Unable to contain her surprise, she asked April what she was doing back in New York. We thought she had planned to stay away for good. April was clearly embarrassed, probably thinking that she had let us down. But what she said was important to our understanding. "When I got back home and got my job, I knew no one would understand what I'd been doing for the past eight years. I also knew that I'd have to create a life in order to explain to the people I used to know where I'd been. So I made up a story which I thought people would believe, and they did. But every time I had to tell that story I felt dead inside. And I felt confused. I just couldn't keep on pretending." Then, pointing up and down the street, she said, "As bad as this life is, and as much shit as I have to take, at least here people know who I am. And so do I."

How could anyone not understand her plight? Afraid to reveal the truth about her life, she fabricated a history and lost her personhood. She needed to return to the streets in order to reclaim it. And in fact April worked almost two more years, until she met Ross. As their relationship blossomed, she continued supporting herself and Ross by turning tricks. In time they decided to get married, and Howard performed the wedding ceremony one sunny spring day in the church garden. After the service, April turned around and said, "You can't possibly understand how important it is to me to be married here, where everyone knows who I am."

Within months, both April and Ross were enrolled in trade schools, and before the year was out she had left the life for good. But she had left with her dignity intact.

From April and Crystal we learned a great deal about the damage done by the square world's attitude toward prostitutes as well as ex-prostitutes. Conditioning teaches them that society will refuse to recognize their humanity, a belief that has a foundation in reality. Take, for example, a group like Women Against Pornography, in its New York manifestation. Founded in the late 1970s by Susan Brownmiller, author of *Against Our Will,* it is the outgrowth of several predecessor organizations made up of liberal feminists. Groups of women who were joined together in their opposition to rape eventually formed organizations with a broader general concern about all violence directed at women. By the time Brownmiller and her colleagues founded WAP, its appeal was so great that it found itself attracting members from the politically conservative religious right. The focus of WAP's energies is the control and/or elimination of pornography, which, they believe, represents a hatred of women, expressed through the degradation and humiliation of women's bodies for the pleasure of male consumers. WAP maintains that such "exploitation" is the "cause" of violence directed against women.

As the WAP campaign developed, part of the strategy was to take groups of citizens on educational tours of peep shows and "dirty" book stores in the Times Square area. They even published a map which indicated the location of those establishments, along with one added feature: the addresses of "brothels" in Times Square. The birth of WAP conveniently coincided with the "cleanup" campaign of the Mayor's Task Force, which had begun the systematic raiding and closing down of massage parlors in Manhattan. WAP became the instrument that protected the mayor and his lieutenants from being accused of antifeminist activity. In exchange, an abandoned storefront in Times Square was given to WAP to use as their headquarters. WAP members often bragged about the pressure they brought on the city to close down brothels and the influence they had with the authorities.

Arlene decided to join one of the tours. The group was led to a building on Forty-second Street where a massage parlor rented space. The leader made an impassioned speech about why the city should close it down. WAP was going after brothels because it was believed that the women employees were exploited sexually and financially by male management and customers. After all, the leader claimed, the women had no health insurance or other benefits. WAP was "concerned" about the dreadful working conditions and was trying to help the women by forcing them out of jobs.

It was all reminiscent of the infancy of the women's movement in the late 1960s, when, at a conference on women and work, feminists raged against their middle- and upper-class sisters for employing maids. Housework was thought to be a degrading and humiliating occupation, and women hired for that purpose were exploited by their employers. At that gathering, a group of minority women confronted the white leadership and in very clear and unmistakable terms told them to mind their own business. Until the women's movement could come up with alternative employment for those whose only occupational option was housework, they should save their preaching. For the present, it was housework that put food on the table, and white women couldn't know what it was like to live on the edge of survival. Only the absence of such understanding allowed them to call so casually for the elimination of a profession that enabled some of their sisters to keep families clothed and sheltered.

The question of prostitution is not really very different. WAP claims that so long as there are prostitutes selling their bodies, men will continue to see all women as whores. Pornography and prostitution are related wings of an industry that should be eliminated, as the cause of violence toward women. WAP's "holier than thou" posture ignores the disruption this would create in the lives of women working in the sex industry. Be they prostitutes or peep-show dancers, these women will be put out of work if their places of employment are shut down. Perhaps WAP thinks it better that they and their children try to survive on welfare. At least the women won't suffer the indignity of being exploited as sex objects!

The reaction of many prostitutes to the WAP philosophy is interesting. They see themselves as providing men with an outlet for sexual frustration and thereby *preventing* rapes. As sexual surrogates—even social workers—they cool down men who have reached the boiling point. If their services were not available, they believe, violence would, ironically, be directed toward women like those who belong to WAP.

When WAP first received public attention, many who work the peep shows and streets of Times Square were horrified and hurt that a group of women would organize around putting them out of work. They had always known that men were the enemy; women disrupting sex shows while leading tours, and urging authorities to close down massage parlors, came as a shock. If any women had been perceived as enemies, it was suburban housewives, middle-aged and middle class, who were threatened by the freedom to express oneself sexually which had come into fashion in the 1960s. Workers in the sex industry didn't expect their contemporaries to come down on them. After all, these were the same women who fought for the right to control their own bodies when the abortion issue was the center of a national debate. Weren't prostitutes, in their work, living out that conviction?

Fortunately, there is disagreement within the women's movement over the issue of prostitution. Some feminist organizations, like the National Organization of Women, stand in favor of the decriminalization of prostitution. And younger groups, like Feminists Against Censorship Taskforce (FACT), have begun to dispute the claims and charges of WAP. In addition, lesbians and gay men individually and organizationally are among the strongest supporters of the rights of prostitutes to work safely and securely. Those who see themselves under attack for their own sexuality and who are still fighting for their own rights have been quick to identify with another oppressed minority. They believe their rights are intimately entwined with the rights of prostitutes.

All of the Judson women who participated in our venture on the streets were deeply affected by their exposure to prostitutes. None could deny that they were ordinary and likable human beings. Expectations of differences went unfulfilled. Instead there were feelings of identification, friendship, and concern. Here are some more passages from their journal:

> There was a brouhaha over a customer who wanted to shoot up in the room while being given a blow job. Mindy turned the customer down, but Toya agreed to go with him. This angered the other women, who felt Toya's actions endangered them all. There was some talk of telling the parlor manager what Toya was doing, but it was vetoed. . . .
>
> I asked Ruby how long she'd been working. She said only for a week on the street, that usually she does body rubs, dances, etc.

Then she asked me how long I'd been working. I said I didn't and told her a little about why we were there. She said, "You're crazy. You know you'll get busted too. They don't care if you're just standing there—they'll pick you up. It happened to me once." I said we knew that was always a possibility. She shook her head and said again, "You're crazy."

She told me that three days ago her mother found her on Eighth Avenue, and though she told her that she was merely waiting for someone, she thinks her mother knows the truth and that she has really suspected her daughter was a prostitute for some time. Ten years ago Ruby's father abandoned her mother, leaving her the sole support of four daughters, and Ruby says that her mother worked as a waitress but some nights she came home with $100, so now Ruby thinks her mother might have really been a prostitute. . . .

Shortly after we got back, a guy came up to me and asked if I wanted to go out. Toya overheard and got a kick out of it. She told Mindy and they both laughed, saying I could have made some money. . . .

Simone borrowed my umbrella because it is littler and prettier than hers. She's very cute and solicits very nicely. Mindy also solicits very openly and pleasantly, I thought. She spoke some about the men she talked to and one she caught. She is very funny to listen to. . . .

When I got back to "our block" the cop was gone and some women I didn't know were in our spot. I took up my usual place anyway. Seconds later I was alone again and confused. One of the pimps called out to me to move because there was a camera. I went over to stand next to him with my back to the street. Minutes later a cop started coming from the Forty-fourth Street end and the man I was standing next to was making remarks about what was I trying to do, and I said, "Stay out of trouble," and I guess he realized again that I didn't know what was happening and said, "Cop." I turned and looked and the policeman was only a few feet away from me. I was afraid to walk too close in front of him so I walked past him, crossed Forty-fourth Street and then up the other side of the street. I felt exhausted and so I walked up to the parlor at Forty-sixth Street, went in, sat down, and had a cigarette. The women there are so friendly that it was like going home. . . .

Paulette told us about being beat up the night before with the police standing across the street watching, but offering no assistance. She said another woman had the same experience, with the police offering no aid. . . .

A number of men propositioned us or spoke to us. One woman asked if we got many offers and what we said. She then asked if we were "for or against" the women and Arlene said that we were for all women being free to live as they wished.

The conversation turned to police harassment and Mary's man pointed out large scabs on her elbows, commenting that the ones on her knees were even worse. He said they were the result of a fall she took while running away from the cops. She said there was one cop in the precinct who threatened to crack her head open with his night stick if he ever caught her walking there again and another who had warned her that he was out to get her sexually and one night was going to pick her up so he could have her. . . .

Since the streets were deserted except for the cops, we decided to go to the coffee shop for something cool to drink. We began to discuss my feeling about Tuesday night, particularly the implication that the cop would apologize for hurting me—a last, lingering feeling that I was different (better?) than the other women.

Let us now look at the men in a prostitute's life, and the variety of ways they see her. Since we deal with pimps and police elsewhere, we will omit those categories.

First, we have to examine the "trick," upon whom she is dependent for her livelihood and with whom she forms a temporary symbiotic relationship. What they have in common is their need of each other, and that is about as far as it goes. But the trick's need for the prostitute is considered *normal*—the male in our society is expected to have a large sexual appetite and to spend time seeking its fulfillment. So men can purchase recreational sex without much fear of being castigated by society or arrested by the police.

This double standard relates to an issue that sporadically surfaces in the area of law enforcement—the discriminatory application of the solicitation law. Since obviously men are breaking the same law, they should be subject to the same punishment, yet the solicitation law is invoked only to arrest women. Historically, this cause was one of the first that occupied the feminist movement as it sought to liberate and seek equality for women who were working as prostitutes. It was believed that if customers were arrested with the same frequency as prostitutes, the laws would be changed. The movement, however, came up against the hard reality of "selective enforcement" on the part of the police, and learned that the wording of the law—however clear its statement that purveyors and purchasers of sex are equally subject to arrest and prosecution—has very little to do with the way in which it is applied.

One night Howard was standing on the street near where we were visiting with the women. A policeman approached and cautioned him to move along, saying it was an area where prostitutes were picked up. He clearly thought that Howard (who was not wearing a clerical collar) was looking for a proposition, and his warning was certainly a courtesy seldom extended to the women who were working.

Egalitarians, in their push for nondiscriminatory application of the law, mistakenly believed that prostitutes would be grateful for this show of support. Actually, they were very much against customers' being arrested, because the women would thereby suffer double jeopardy—going to jail and losing customers, who would be afraid to risk arrest.

Even apart from the prostitutes' self-interest, equal prosecution of men and women may not make a lot of sense. If the present law is unjust, and perhaps unconstitutional, why should it be compounded by penalizing the customer and threatening his livelihood and family structure? It would only prove that injustice is indiscriminate. A few years ago, the mayor of New York very straightforwardly expressed his willingness to expose men who were visiting prostitutes, and to use the city radio station to that end. The mayor would have broadcast the names of arrested "johns" as though this great cosmopolitan capital of the world were a midwestern village with strict sexual mores.

There is another problem if one wants to take seriously the issue of indiscriminate application. That is the immense number of men involved. The male population of New York City over twenty-one years of age is near 2.5 million. If one extrapolates from the Kinsey studies, some 1.5 million of these visit prostitutes at least once in their life and approximately 800,000 visit them periodically. Consider the harvest of arrests if the law were applied equally in regard to customers!

It may be hard to bear, but with working women we face the most blatant kind of double standard. Engaging in the same activity, a woman is called "whore" and "slut," while a man is named a "Don Juan" or "gigolo." Society labels the woman's behavior "deviant" and "criminal" and the male's behavior normal. From this labeling alone the trick develops a sense of superiority over the women he patronizes. Statistical studies have shown who the male customers are: the average trick is white, male, married, between the ages of twenty-five and forty-five. These largely middle- and upper-middle-class customers see themselves as purchasing sexual services from women who are of a lower class, much as many of us might judge a person who collects garbage as lower class. The service being offered determines the judgment. Further, the working woman is a female outside the family system, and therefore considered abnormal. Add to this that she can be "bought," and we have sufficient grounds for feelings of superiority and scorn toward those women who trade in sexual services in order to make a living.

Apart from this disrespect, there is hardly any way for us to understand the bartering that goes on between tricks and prostitutes in establishing the price for the service. Though the customer feels that the loathsome act of the prostitute is something he wouldn't do for all the money in the world, nevertheless, no matter how reasonable her price, he wants the service for less. This devaluation of the work is there in spite of the fact that many customers, as is clear from the women's storytelling, are impotent or sexually dysfunctional with their wives or lovers.

One reason so many married males seek out prostitutes is not that they are unhappily married or that their marriage is breaking up, but rather that they are pleasured by forms of sexual action, such as oral-genital sex, in which their wives will not engage or which they cannot bring themselves to ask for. This is more true of an older generation, whose freedom of sexual activity was more restricted. Some men see visiting a prostitute as a less offensive infidelity than becoming involved with a nonprostitute, which might lead to a rupture in the marriage. At the same time, they resent their need to do this.

These feelings of the customer can degenerate easily into hostility when complicated by other emotions. An otherwise normal male seeking out and propositioning a prostitute may experience a feeling of real inferiority. There is guilt that as a happily married man or successful lover, he somehow is dependent on this woman of the streets. Deep resentment may accompany a realization that he has to pay for what other men obtain free. So though he perceives the prostitute as less than human, he also sees her as a professional able to do for him what other women can't. The result is that he views her at best with ambivalence and at worst with anger. We shouldn't be surprised, therefore, that she risks greater violence at the hands of the trick than of her pimp. The experience of the women we observed bore this out.

In examining this complex symbiosis between prostitute and customer, we could regard prostitution as another "service" in a society that puts so high a value on service. The service that is paid for is care. The prostitute's service is not care in any profound sense, but then neither is the service of many doctors, lawyers, and teachers. Her service, rather, is limited to a somewhat modest demand—sexual satisfaction, usually restricted to the pleasure of an orgasm. (Perhaps our inability to accept prostitution as part of our way of life is to some degree founded on its identification with personal pleasure or self-indulgence and its lack of utilitarian value.)

However, society does accept other forms of sexual transactions that satisfy the criteria of service, and these have been historically approved, if not officially condoned. For example, the medical profession employs sexual surrogates to work with patients who demonstrate certain types of sexual dysfunction. In this instance we withhold our condemnation because the sex for pay serves a "higher goal." Or take prostitution and penology: Men incarcerated in segregated facilities for long periods have sometimes been offered the company of single women who "service" prisoners. This is done to "sustain morale," prevent violent outbreaks, and perhaps curb homosexual rape. It again seems clear that prostitution as a service dedicated to a "nobler" cause is acceptable. In the armed forces, particularly in wartime, prostitution may be an aid to troop morale and becomes an acceptable "mission" for women who deal in sexual services. Closely allied to this is another patriotic justification, women espionage agents who use their sexual wiles for extracting information from the enemy. Mata Haris have been heroines of the spy world and staples of literature throughout the ages. It is important to recognize how we make prostitution palatable or even glamorous if it is offered in the service of a cause. Somehow our judgment is softened when we think of the prostitute servicing, for example, severely handicapped persons (particularly paraplegic veterans of the Vietnam War) whose opportunities to develop more normal relationships with women have been seriously limited. Occasionally, on the street, a blind person is led to where the women are to negotiate the purchase of sex.

Without knowing the strange or even kinky requests that customers make of prostitutes, it is difficult for the general public to understand why one speaks of the prostitute as meeting needs and being a sexual therapist of sorts. One of the more poignant stories concerned a date one woman saw as often as he had enough money to buy her services. All he wanted was for the woman to bite him on the neck in a very visible place, so that his friends and colleagues would think that he had a girlfriend who found him irresistible. One night he was pointed out to us, and while he was homely in appearance, there was nothing about him physically that suggested he would need to go to a prostitute. Nevertheless he believed himself unable to engage in a sexual relationship with a "square" woman because he was unattractive.

Then there was the diaper man, a handsome young customer known to many of the women. He rarely went with the same woman more than once. He would pay twenty-five dollars to have his diaper changed. (He always wore one on these occasions and carried a fresh one with him.)

And also, though it may seem a bit dated, there are still fathers who take their sons to visit a prostitute on their eighteenth birthday for their sexual rite of passage. As she told of a kid who came to her for such an initiation, one woman's harsh and cynical speech softened, her gruffness vanished, as she explained how gentle, relaxed, and caring she was with him. She seemed to understand that this first sexual experience could affect all future relationships.

Among tricks in general, there is a very particular kind of customer, known in the business as a "regular." Women would be sitting on the bus carrying on an intense conversation about the new cop on the beat or the new wife-in-law, when suddenly one of them would jump from her seat as if wired for an alarm, and leave, explaining, "It's my regular." We learned that the regular is a very special customer to a working woman. Married or single, he seeks her out once or twice a week. Generally she has known and served him over a period of time; he usually pays better than transient tricks; and ordinarily he is dependable.

When things are slow and there's not too much business, the sight of a regular can make a woman's week. These men have been known to give women large amounts of money, and with them the professionals don't run the clock. "Normal" sexual relations are more likely. The regular may come for sexual satisfactions or pleasures that he cannot get in a conventional relationship. He establishes a bond with the working woman, and mutuality of need usually makes them dependent on each other: he needs her services and she needs the money he pays. It is among regulars that working women many times find a husband when they are ready to square up and move out of the life.

Sam is a doctor, affiliated with a large suburban hospital. He is forty-two years old, divorced, a fine-looking, cultured person. He had been one of Angel's regulars for several years. Weekly visits with her became very important to him, and he finally decided to pursue her, hoping she would leave the life and marry him. One day he called us at Judson to say how much he admired the work we were doing with prostitutes and that he was sending a generous donation in her name. Angel had left the life and he had tried, with no success, to find out where she was. He told us how much he respected and loved her.

On occasion we were truly amazed to discover who some of the women's tricks were. The first time this happened was when Muffin returned to New York City from an extended stay in Albany. As she was explaining the differences between working on Eighth Avenue and in the state capital, we casually asked if she ever dated politicians. She said she did. Like who? we asked. Muffin then named a high-level lawmaker, mispronouncing his name and seeming not to know just how important a public official he was. Stunned, we asked how she could be sure it was him. With downcast eyes, she said, "Because I stole his gold American Express card." This was not the last occasion when we discovered that some of the men who make the laws that criminalize women are themselves lawbreakers.

There is another kind of trick who sees the women from time to time on a business basis, but men in this category are really "street people" who are buddies with the women. Albert was on the street every night, watching the scene. He knew all the women by name and was a kind of patron/trick to several, whom he had tried to help from time to time. When one of the women was in the hospital, he would send her small gifts. Albert spent his days at the racetrack and his evenings on the street. His money came from horses and not from any illicit trade. He took a genuine and special interest in the welfare of the women, and was a constant presence through the years.

Another such sojourner of the street was the "man without a name." Whenever we were out on the street, in whatever area, he would appear. He was black, wore dark glasses, dressed comfortably but not ostentatiously. He carried a large flight bag over his shoulder. Never speaking, never approaching the women, he would stand at a distance and wait for the women to come to him. Eventually we learned that he was the "rubber man," who supplied them with condoms; he charged a fair price and was always around. One woman told us he was working his way through college. He treated the women with the friendly respect of any salesman.

There are any number of men who seem to treat the women with respect, if not approval, without expecting anything in return. There are the Greyhound and Trailways bus drivers on Eleventh Avenue who allow the women to use the bathrooms on their idle buses, or let them take a quick nap. There are the taxi drivers, many of whom are probably closer to procurer/ friends than anything else. They bring customers to the women and they also transport the women home. On Eighth Avenue on a cold night they will be double parked, letting the women warm up and have a few minutes of friendly conversation. There is also the nutrition freak, who wants the women to pay attention to their diet. He believes that in their work and with their life-style, it is important to look after their health. Though the women think him a bit of a "kook," they are touched by his solicitous concern, and grateful for the vitamins he regularly supplies free of charge.

To explore fully the importance of the views of others toward prostitutes, we must look at the attitude of the society (the collective view) as represented by the law. All one has to do is remember when abortion was a criminal act, as well as an ethical and emotional strain on women with problem pregnancies. Or when homosexuality was both an unacceptable deviancy and a criminal act. The psychic damage done to women who had abortions and to homosexual men and lesbian women was immeasurable. When these behaviors were no longer stigmatized by society and labeled as criminal, much of the psychological impairment that was attributed to having an abortion or being a homosexual was found to be due to the way in which education, law, and medicine treated these persons. One can be sure, for example, that when the American Psychiatric Association declared that homosexuality was no longer a "sickness," a great burden was lifted from those previously so branded. The labeling of the law and the punishing by society are still incredible detriments to the prostitute's being able to find self-affirmation for her existence as a woman.

The insults from dissatisfied customers, the epithets of angry cops—these go with the territory, but what would be welcome from strangers and those who have no contact with the working women is to be treated with a little more deference and a recognition that all of us, prostitute and nonprostitute alike, are on a difficult journey, and all of us need a little understanding and caring.

5

"Me and My People": Primitive Patriarchy in the Modern World

Yesterday,
Love came to me
Without a script.
No index pointing
To rules of
Proper form.
Giving was spontaneous.
Without fear
Faith and devotion
Turning me to you
But . . .
That was yesterday,
Before all directions
I felt were mine
Seemed to unscramble
And picture another
Vision of a
Psychic game
Of parallel words
Coming from another
Body and
Coming from another
Mind.
—DIANE

There is no way to understand prostitutes in any depth without knowing the meaning to them of the words "me and my people." Her "people" is the primary locus of the prostitute's life outside of work; it is this subterranean world's version of "home and hearth," the illicit subculture's own "nuclear family." It may be peopled with babies, small children, and other women, but the centrifugal force of that group is "the man": the nigger, the gentleman of leisure, the player, or, as society likes to label him, the pimp.

In the categories of villains and undesirables in our culture, the pimp is the ultimate "badass." The reasons for this are complicated, but they have a great deal to do with myths and stereotypes, as they do with the prostitute. From what we see and read in media portrayals, the pimp is always Mr. Mean, who preys on unhappy girls who've run away from home, or is a sadistic woman-beater who chains his woman to the life from which there is no escape. He is a conniving dope dealer whom the prostitute clings to out of fear for her life.

It will be helpful first to demythologize the pimp in terms of media and middle-class stereotyping. First we must make a point about judgments of the pimp derived from another culture, using the values and criteria of that culture. The pimp is not the only victim of stereotyping; we do the same to poor blacks, religious fanatics, and homosexuals. It is a labeling process, a simple method of putting people in a place where we can understand, judge, and more often than not, condemn them for their nonconformist life-style or immoral practices. In this way the pimp as a category of human being suffers the same fate as other members of deviant or minority subcultures in our society.

In dealing with the stereotypes, it is important to note two kinds: one is a false perception, and the other is a reality, tolerated in the dominant culture but condemned in the subculture.

One false perception holds that the pimp catches dates, or rounds up tricks, for his woman. This myth probably comes from the definition of the pimp as a "procurer" for prostitutes. Nothing could be further from the truth. Unless "the man" is suspicious of an "early turn-out" or he thinks his "bottom woman" is holding out on him, he is probably drinking with the boys, "having a blow" (cocaine), setting up another business, or taking care of the kids at home. Another such myth is that the pimp is the "protector" of the woman, that anyone who lays a hand on her is as good as dead. If that were true, there wouldn't be so many incidences of prostitutes being beaten, crippled, and killed by tricks and others. One of the first things a woman has to learn on the street is how to care for herself, with a little help from her friends. She cannot count on any strong arm of "her man" to defend her against the daily dangers of violence against her person. Part of her gaining favor in her pimp's eyes is that she can take care of herself: avoid violence, escape police, recognize perverse tricks, get out of jail and back to work without his having to move a hand.

Another of the myths is that the pimp is the primary reason for a woman's being in the life. Either by the use or threat of physical violence or by the power of psychological manipulation, "the man" "turns her out," and she becomes a professional prostitute. This fits the movie and magazine stories, and also our own need to see the pimp as the ultimate villain and the woman as the mistreated or misled victim of her man. It accords with stereotypes of women as weak, male dominated, and highly malleable creatures.

We remember one night when some of the women were talking about how they got into the life. Of about a dozen women, all but one said they did it on their own or at the suggestion and with the help of a girlfriend. Only one said she was "turned out" by her man. Certainly the popular conception is the opposite; to counter it, we present some of the women's replies to Arlene's question: "Were you forced into the life by a pimp?"

Many people say every woman, or most, are forced to become a prostitute. Most girls do it for love. Most girls were young when they started, and the idea of money and living good was a thrill. No one that I know has ever told me they were forced to start. They mostly all met the guy, liked him, and then started. No one, in my opinion, can really be forced to do anything; if they are, there is always a way out. (Shannon)

No, I wasn't forced! It all started when one of my girlfriends was working. We used to sit down and talk about what she was doing. She used to tell me about how much money she was making and the things she used to do, and I started thinking about the money I didn't have. And then one day my man asked me to go to work, and I said "no" for two years. Then I did. It's not as bad as when you read it. It's a beautiful life. You get to meet all kinds of people. I've been working for nine years and living very good. (Gerie)

No, I came into the life of pros through greed, fascination, and thinking I was slick. Pimps come into the picture because your average man thinks that a pros is beneath your square woman and treats her as such. A pros is still a woman, still has needs like any other woman, and a certain breed of man has the aptitude to prey on this—hence pimps. (Crazy Sherry)

I became a prostitute because of family problems long before I even knew a pimp. I had to borrow from my neighbor because my mother didn't give me any money. As a teenager I wanted to go places and party and hang out with my friends, and I didn't have the money or the clothes. I didn't want to borrow or steal because then I would be committing a crime. (Ta-Neisha)

I was all by myself, had nowhere to go. I was hungry, couldn't go home, and I had no money to eat or live. So I came on the streets and started working to make some money, and now I'm not hungry and have a place to live. No one had to put me on the streets. The money is cool, but at least I don't have to be hungry or sleep on the streets, or worry about

*where my next meal is coming from, or where I'm going to
sleep.* (Vickie)

*I was not forced. I liked my man, so I did it. Before I met my
man, I was living on welfare and got a job in a legit massage
parlor in Pennsylvania (not like the ones here in New York).
Only massages. A guy offered me twenty dollars for an extra
deal and I did it. Two years later I met my man and he told
me how nice New York was and how the money was. So I
came here four years ago and have been with him ever since.
I love him. He did not force me. Whatever I don't want to do,
I don't!—P.S. ninety percent for love, ten percent other reasons.* (Name Withheld)

*No, that isn't true at all, it's all fiction or TV action. Now,
what happened in my case—it was mostly out of curiosity
and a lack of funds. It's hard finding a job these days with
just a high school diploma, so you take the most profitable
way out. Now, there is a man involved in my life. I wouldn't
call him my pimp—he's my man. A pimp is something cold
and hard. My man is warm, and if I didn't want to go out and
work, he would not force me. It's up to me, because if I were
forced, I could just as well call the police—they have a pimp
squad for that. So you see, it's almost impossible for someone
to force you to sell your body. There are just too many people
out here to protect you from it.* (Meechie)

*No, it was by choice. The fascination of having money. Then
I fell in love. I'm still in love. It's not all that bad. And people
not in this life cannot conceive it. All they believe in is their
fairy tale ideas of it, with unhappy endings.* (Nikki Mae)

*No. The reason why I became a prostitute is because of the
money. I could not find a job and I needed money. And my
man, he doesn't force me to come out on the streets—it's*

*because I want to. I find it's an easier way to make a living
and to have more things out of life. I was never forced into
prostitution. If I don't want to come out, he doesn't make me.
I'd rather work the streets and get all the things I want.*
(Blanche)

This myth about the pimp pushing women into the life is
closely related to another stereotype—that the pimp chooses
the woman he wants for "his stable," and when he says "I
want," she comes to him. However, the woman more often than
not chooses the man she wants to be with and give her money
to. Many times on the street, we hear of women who leave one
pimp for another. Or a woman with no man decides to work for
a pimp she wants. Conventional wisdom would dictate that
such actions would end in the woman being murdered or
maimed, or she would never work again, but this does not
happen. There may be an occasional pimp who is insanely jealous and wants to punish, but that is rare. The pimp knows that
uncertainty is part of the game he is playing, and is to be expected. There is even a code that if a woman chooses another
man, that is to be respected, and if her first man harms her, he
will have to answer to the new man in her life.

Now let's turn to the second stereotype that is fairly common
currency—the use of a different set of criteria for members of
a subculture than for members of the dominant culture. So that
behavior in a pimp which is judged unacceptable is deemed
acceptable, if tasteless, in a member of the majority culture. In
dealing with "deviant subcultures," it is known as the double-
standard judgment. An illustration: "Pimps indulge in an ostentatious display of the material benefits of their profession." An
Upper West Side liberal deplores the presence of prostitutes in
the neighborhood because they bring "those disgusting pimps
with their purple Cadillacs and mink coats and big diamonds on
their fingers, flaunting the rewards of their business. We don't
want people like that in our neighborhood." How would this

West Sider have felt if the intruder were not a local pimp but a Walt Frazier or another superstar of our culture? Isn't it strange that a red Eldorado with a white vinyl top is called a "pimpmobile" when driven by a black man, but a gray Continental with a white man behind the wheel is seen as elegant wealth? Could it be true that even our aesthetics are tinged with racial and class bias? It's also interesting to observe who tolerates such behavior—the poor people in the ghetto love it, the middle class abhors it, and the rich endure it.

If we explore intolerance of the pimp's behavior, I think we will discover that the hostility is about the fact that he doesn't do anything for the money he receives. In other words, he doesn't work for his pay; women do the labor, and he collects. But in our economic culture, don't we find that there are people, certain kinds of middlemen, making money off other people's labor? They don't do anything but lift up the phone once in a while. Like the Hollywood agents who get their percentage from the labors of film stars, or the reputable agencies that sell models' bodies to magazines, fashion shows, or the Seventh Avenue merchandisers. Or, on a less glamorous level, the employment or apartment agencies that make a bundle by brokering information.

We all know that there are double standards, but we don't always know when we're using them. When a pimp assaults his woman, it makes headlines and is called wanton brutality, but every day in our square life husbands beat their wives, and we call it a sickness which needs to be helped.

Perhaps the most common image carried of the pimp is that he is an unconscionable parasite living off the drudgery and hardship of others. Even if that were a completely correct view of him, when we think of how many people (lawyers, doctors, drug manufacturers, crutch makers, therapists, to name only a few) live off the misery, sickness, and hardships of others, it would seem that the public judgment reveals at least another double standard. Incidentally, there is a further illustration of the double standard operating on the pimp. Historically speaking, probably prior to pimps in commercialized prostitution, the "madam" in a bordello lived off the prostitutes' earnings. The madam, like the pimp, was a friend and exploiter of the prostitutes' work, yet she never bore the same stigma. It may be that her press was not as bad because she was a woman, but it probably has much more to do with the fact that the pimp is black and his women are so often white.

If one pretended that it is just coincidence that 99 percent of pimps are black, it would be just as naive to assume it accidental that blacks predominate in boxing, basketball, baseball, and football. It's interesting that pimps think of their work as a "game," and that another name for prostitution is "sportin' life," in which the pimp is a "player."

But what the white majority admires on the playing fields of America it downright detests in the arena of sex. It would be naive indeed to assume that race and, particularly, the long, arduous, sometimes ugly relationship between black and white in America and the racism spawned by that history do not play a role in prostitution. If we pretended that some of the hostility and abhorrence shown the pimp does not stem from the fact that he has crossed over the sacrosanct barrier of sexuality with white women, we would be closing our eyes.

History is never dead for black Americans. They remember that in times of slavery white masters raped black women with impunity, but also that some black women cooperated with white masters to gain a more secure place. And white masters socially castrated black men by not allowing them to be heads of their own households, and denied them access to white women. If their historical memory serves them right, then the black pimp has reversed history. He is dominant over black *and* white women. (Isn't it interesting that we have called prostitution "white slavery"?) Now white men suffer the ignominious put-down of having to pay white women for sexual favors that go to the black man free and easy. The pimp not only crossed over the sex line with white women, but he also humiliated the white man by making him pay for what his women lavishly give the black man.

There are whole theses and books on this subject, but this is just a reminder that where pimps are concerned in our society, we are not simply dealing with practitioners of a sordid profession or with class snobbishness, but confronting an unspoken black racial component that is nowhere more resented and abhorred than when it is mixed with a sexual component. Racial discrimination in the work life and in the ghetto gave birth to this profession that so outrages us. However, more important than the racial factor is the self-image of the man, the way he perceives himself in the relationship with the prostitute: rather differently than we who are looking at him from the outside.

The prostitute's man does not recognize himself in the badass stereotype by which he is caricatured in the square world. He doesn't see himself as an enslaver of women; he rather thinks of himself as a business entrepreneur. Indeed, that is one of the roles the pimp plays. He is not "playing around with sex" so much as he is running a small business—the merchandise is recreational sex, and he organizes, directs, and collects from one or more women who are the salespeople of sex. At least part of the time, he thinks of these women as employees rather than as sex objects or lovers. In his business role, he demands of his workers certain hours on the job—they are not judged by piecework but by how much money they bring in on a weekly basis.

He also imposes certain work standards: his employee must stay off drugs and alcohol while on the job. As a matter of fact, behavior such as excessive coffee-klatching or goofing off is considered bad conduct, for which the women may be dressed down or penalized. When we first took our mobile unit out, some pimps forbade their women to come on the bus while they were working, partly because they didn't know us but more because it would take time from work, and therefore their earnings. Later, when women were arrested because they weren't on the bus, the men changed their tune. The pimp can be as tough and demanding as any other employer who doesn't have a union to deal with, one for whom hours, time off, and pay are not subject to collective bargaining. He usually chooses to pay the woman in goods and services rather than cash, providing her clothes, jewelry, food, housing, and per diem allowance. Insofar as the pimp takes care of business, he thinks of himself as an entrepreneur.

One of the more unusual pimps we came to know was not satisfied merely to pay for his women's clothes. He designed and made them as well. His women are among the best-dressed prostitutes working on the East Side, and whenever we complimented one on her outfit she would explain that E. deserved all the credit.

The pimp enacts a multifaceted role in relating to his woman or women. If the man were only a "businessman," a whip-cracking employer, he wouldn't keep the women long at all. He is and has to be much more. He has to be everything to a woman. When he scolds her because she had her money stolen or sassed a cop and got booked, he becomes a father correcting his wayward daughter. When he is protective and admiring as she relates how she took a knife to a mean transvestite, he becomes a brother. When he is listening to her reactions to an overbearing wife-in-law and the injustices of her work situation, and counsels her on her attitudes, he becomes her therapist. And last, and probably least, when he romantically sweet-talks her and takes her to bed (his most infrequent role, if the women's testimony means anything), then he is her lover.

One of the least attractive prostitutes we ever met has been with her man for over five years. By her own testimony, they *never* have sex, yet she seems untroubled by this and remains absolutely loyal. She is aware that he does make love to her wife-in-law (who recently bore his child), but claims not to be disturbed by this inequity. When she gets horny, she disappears for a few days with some guy or another, but then faithfully returns to her man.

Perhaps the most important role is assumed when the relationship becomes stable and long-lasting, and the pimp takes a woman to meet his mom or the grandmother who raised him; then he plays the role of husband. This does not happen with great frequency because there are instances where the pimp's mother involves herself in his business, encouraging him to retire his woman and settle down to a square life. When that occurs, it puts ideas in his woman's head, creating problems in their relationship which he would rather avoid dealing with.

The only joy and pleasure, to a prostitute who loves her man, that means more than "going home" is to bear his child or legally marry him. That, to the woman, is the final affirmation of his love for her, and she thinks little of whether it will be any more durable than a marriage in the "square world." As with all of us "normal" people, to her the odds don't matter!

Another of the pimp's roles in his professional life, albeit perhaps an inadvertent one, is that of model for ghetto youth. Until recently, it wasn't easy for the young, street-wise, unemployed ghetto kid to see anything resembling a model of material attainment, particularly if he had no athletic talent. You may protest that there are plenty of black computer executives, schoolteachers, and social workers, but they don't usually go back to the old neighborhood, and hardly any of them earn $100,000 a year plus, drive a custom Caddy, and "blow coke" at will. We who draw our values from the majority culture may find this model unattractive, but we ought to understand its appeal among young people whose unemployment rate is approximately 49 percent and for whom urban summer work brings $3.50 an hour. Here is a man who looks good, goes to Florida or Puerto Rico in the winter, drives a fancy car, and takes in up to six figures a year in nontaxable earnings, and the only training he had for the job was the hustling street smarts that every ghetto survivor possesses.

To dispel the too easy stereotypes of pimps prevalent in popular images as constructed by the various media, we feel it would be helpful to draw impressionistic characterizations of pimps we have known. It would be less than candid if we gave the impression that we had any kind of in-depth relationship with these men, and in at least one instance we know them more through their women than through direct experience.

Big Lou was the first pimp we ever knew. We met him on Eighth Avenue in 1976. He ran an adult porno shop with XXX-rated movies in the front and a "massage parlor" in the back.

Big Lou lived up to his name. He was some six feet three inches tall and weighed about 225 pounds, and his towering physique made you feel small and fearful, but the gentleness of the man calmed the fear and set you at ease. His skin was as black as the mud of South Carolina, where he grew up, and he had a smile that could light up Times Square. He dressed casually and seemed to shun the red-hot superfly image of other pimps.

We heard about Lou long before we met him. He was held in high regard by the women and had a reputation for helping many of them through difficult periods in their lives without ever asking to be paid or expecting the women to work for him.

Janice told us how she met Lou shortly after she arrived in New York at the age of fourteen. She had run away from the foster family she had been living with for three years, and in order to support herself had begun to turn tricks. Her foster father had abused her sexually, so she knew there was a market. When Lou saw her on the street one night, he realized she was just a kid. Troubled by the thought of what might happen, he persuaded Janice to go home with him. She stayed for four years. In that time she baby-sat for his children, and Lou never put a hand on her. Janice's gratitude was so great that she said she'd give her life for him. And she was not the only woman who felt that way.

One of our first contacts with Lou came through a most unlikely incident which became a legend on the street, and later was confirmed by Father Bruce Ritter in one of his fund-raising letters for Under 21. In 1976 this organization opened up across

the street from Big Lou's massage parlor and advertised that it
was going to save young kids from the "garbage heap of porno,
prostitution and drugs that is Eighth Avenue."

In spite of Father Ritter's hostility, Big Lou took up a collection from the women who frequented his place, to contribute
to a cause he agreed with. (What happened with the collection
is reported elsewhere.) Lou believed that underaged girls were
in danger on the street and should be sheltered and counseled.
It is an attitude shared by working women, and when they find
someone too young and naive, they give the kid a hard time,
encouraging her to go home.

Big Lou's concern was not limited to an occasional act of
charity. He expressed regularly his fear for the women who
worked the streets. He believed them to be in danger, as indeed
they are, and was constantly trying to persuade them to work
inside. We were hard-pressed to explain the rather touching
concern in this semiliterate, street-wise hustler from the Pied-
mont backwaters. We didn't know him long before recognizing
one of the sources, his deeply religious upbringing. His booming
voice would call out, "Hey, Reverend Howard, God bless you,
how you doin'?" He would then launch into a rather impressive
recitation of how the Lord had blessed him lately, as if in confirmation of what his good mother had always said—that if he kept
in touch with the Lord, the Lord would surely bless him. He
would cheerfully confess, "I done told the Lord I'm His, and I'm
gonna live for Him and talk to Him every day."

Our first reaction to these pious remarks from a confirmed
pimp who managed a porno parlor was shocked amusement.
How humorously incongruous, hearing these sanctimonious
words flow from the mouth of an "ungodly sinner" whom most
religious people would condemn as unfit to utter the name of
God, let alone claim His blessing! As time went on, it didn't
sound strange at all, for it was part of his black Southern religious roots, which had taught him at an early age that he was
a child of God even if he was black and poor. No matter what

he did, he belonged to God. There is a little-understood passage in the Scriptures, "God is no respecter of persons," which probably means that pimps, preachers, and politicians can claim the Lord! Lou never seemed to believe that the work he did was an obstacle to his contact with God as long as he was respectful and kind to people, took care of his women, and raised his children in the fear and love of God.

If his religious talk and expressions of faith seemed incongruous to his profession, it was no more so than the fact that this "procurer of women" was a devoted family man. Big Lou had three children—a crawler, a toddler, and a first-grader. The day he took Howard home with him, the housekeeper greeted them at the door as they picked their way through the toys on the floor. The children were beautiful, and Lou beamed as Howard exclaimed over each one of them, and pronounced him fortunate to have such a family. "Reverend Howard," Lou said, growing serious, "the Lord done blessed me with these children and they come first. Ain't nothin'—not my women, nor my work, nothin'—is more important than my children."

With that vow, they left to take his six-year-old to school for a conference with her teacher.

Many women passed in and out of Big Lou's life and work over the ensuing years, but Patsy, the mother of his children, was always there, the "bottom lady" in his life. After the city closed his massage parlor in 1978, we lost touch for a while, but then ran into him on Eighth Avenue. He had a new place; he was running an escort service (drop-in or call-out) in the Broadway area. He was as happy as ever, said the Lord was still blessing him. Patsy was still with him, the children were growing, and business was picking up in spite of police harassment.

What a strange world it seemed. Here was a pimping entrepreneur in the sex business, and his reputation in society's view was the lowest of the low. We were strangely thankful for life's serendipity: that the first real-life pimp we came to know gave lie to all the prejudices we had acquired about his kind. We are

not asserting that Big Lou is not capable of anger, and mistreat-
ment of women, and neglect of his children, or perhaps even
cursing the name of God, but those are weaknesses all men
share. And there is no claim that he is typical of all pimps, but
then, what pimp is?

Dorothy was one of the most beautiful women we ever met
on the street, and we stayed out there long enough to see her
"square up." Her man, with whom she stayed for some five
years, was named Bobby.

They met over rolls of quarters. He worked in a shoe store,
she worked in a boutique next door, and she used to go over for
change. Bobby took to flirting with her, and she was curiously
attracted to him. She guessed (wrongly) that he was Puerto
Rican. He used to tease her, but she found him offensive when
he pinched her. He was slight of stature, had chocolate-colored
skin and an easygoing manner. Dorothy told him he looked as
if he should have been a priest, and he said he was kind of a
priest. He then told her about a bunch of kids he worked with
in the ghetto, raising their consciousness. They had been brain-
washed by the Catholic Church, he said, and he was trying to
rectify all the bad ideas that had been put in their heads.

There wasn't time then to develop a friendship. Dorothy lost
her job, and had a three-month fling at a bad marriage. One day
Bobby called and wanted to get together. He said he had quit
selling shoes and was now a pimp. Dorothy, untutored in the
ways of the world, said, "What's that?" He said that someday he
would tell her. Some months later, Dorothy was living in Boston
with a gay black male model. Bobby came to visit, and she was
glad to see him; the attraction had been slowly growing in her.
They went for a walk and saw prostitutes on the street; Dorothy
asked him what they were doing, and he said, "They are working for a pimp." Dorothy, trying to recover from the shock, said,
"That's what you do?"

A short time later, Dorothy lost her job and her apartment,
and Bobby asked her to come live with him. She accepted, got

a hairdressing job, went to work every day and came home every night. Bobby stayed home and was charming company: he read a lot to her, talked about consciousness raising and some about his Muslim religion. But months went by and he never said anything about her working as a prostitute.

They would have arguments, and he would tell her that her beliefs were naive and unformed, then he would show her all kinds of books, most of them Black Muslim books about white supremacy and the "white devils" who touted it. (Dorothy was white.) One day in a conversation, Bobby asked Dorothy if she agreed that the body is not the soul. Of course she agreed: Man is not body or mind, but soul. Now the logic was leading somewhere. So what does it mean if you take something into your body that gives pleasure to someone else? That logic didn't work with Dorothy. Weeks went by before the subject was raised again. (If nothing else, Bobby was patient.) Then one day Bobby pursued the logic of the body-mind split. If you were hooking for someone whose nature you knew, or for the furtherance of your own divine knowledge, for some higher reason, would it not be acceptable?

Though Dorothy fought the reasoning, she decided against her better judgment to do it. Lured by testing the reality, she went with her first trick. He gave her ninety dollars, and she ran out with the money before he finished. She cried all the way home, charged angrily into the house, and threw the money in Bobby's face, screaming her revulsion. "This is what you want me to do! I thought you loved me!"

Bobby was duly penitent. He said he never thought it would be like that for her, and he did love her. They were reconciled, and months went by with nothing being said about her working. Then a crisis came: There was no money, no food, and Bobby needed funds quickly. They talked about it. He could go out and get a job, or start robbing, which was not in keeping with his character. Dorothy decided she would make another try, and went on the street with a friend of Bobby's. She worked in Chinatown, and though it didn't seem as bad as before, it took its psychological toll. Dorothy felt sullied by the life she was leading. When she bathed, she never could get clean enough. She wouldn't let Bobby touch her. When she expressed her loathing of the work, her man would tell her it was only for a while, until he could get enough money to set up this Black Muslim school in the ghetto for small children. Bobby always met her complaints with philosophical logic, like bad means to attain good ends. All of her rebellions were met with accusations of her transgressions. She was already guilt-ridden, so it wasn't hard to play on these emotions. He added the guilt of racism, raving about persecution by whites: "Sell shoes or shine shoes"—that's all they would let him do. He gave her a bizarre Moorish-American Bible that told the story of how blacks were created first, and they got together with some monkeys and created white piglike humans who were used as slaves by blacks until they rebelled (a real twist on the Christian Bible's story about the sons of Ham, colored, destined to be "hewers of wood and drawers of water"). These stories frightened Dorothy and increased her guilt.

After the first year, Bobby got Dorothy her own apartment. This way, she could bring men home, and he wouldn't have to sleep in the same bed. Oddly enough, Dorothy understood and accepted his revulsion at not wanting to share the bed where she carried on her sex trade. Bobby only showed up to collect the money. By now he knew that Dorothy was hooked—on him, on the black mystique, on her own guilt. He knew she would react like Pavlov's dog. The more money she made, the more he showed up; the less money, the less she saw of him. Nothing more needed to be said.

One day Dorothy had a traumatic experience with a trick. He put a gun to her head, she begged for her life, and he spared her. Freaking out, she called a girlfriend, who took her to Bobby. She told him what had happened, and he fled the house. Dorothy didn't see him for two weeks. Work became increasingly unbearable for her. If a trick made the slightest move, she would collapse. Getting no advice or comfort from Bobby, she decided to try and leave the life. She went to New York and moved in with a cousin. Unable to find other work, she got a job in a massage parlor; she felt safer, more protected there, and her fears subsided.

Bobby had encouraged her to read and she read voraciously. The only books he had not allowed around the house were "psychology" books. But now pop-psych books like *I'm OK— You're OK* began to plant the seeds of rebellion in Dorothy. It was to be some time before they bore fruit.

In a few months, Bobby came to New York, bringing two other women with him; they all moved in with Dorothy and her cousin. She was still working in the parlor, and her "wife-in-laws" made twice as much on the street. A good pimp knows how to pit his women against each other to see who can make the most. The reward was sleeping in the big bed with him. In the early morning when Dorothy came home, she would find herself consigned to a cot under the stairwell. It sounds like a B-movie, but it worked. Dorothy went back to the street and worked compulsively sixteen hours a day, earning five hundred to six hundred dollars a night, and all of it went to Bobby. Dorothy explained her staying with Bobby in a retrospective reminiscence:

> *I know it sounds crazy and maybe it was, but I loved him in my own sick way. He was my whole life. He was my reason for living. I was the kind of person who desperately needed something or someone to live for. You see, I never liked myself or found myself worthy enough to live for. He was the only light in my life.*

It was a poignant confession, but not crazy. It was one that thousands of square middle-class women could identify with.

In the fourth year, Bobby saw *Charlie's Angels* on TV, and

he got better-looking, younger women and took them out to show them off. Bobby played golf every day with upper-middle-class people in a New York suburb, and there would be days when he would take his women to the golf course to exhibit them. The country clubbers knew what Bobby did, and they were titillated by this brief shoulder-rubbing with another world, but Dorothy hated it.

As time went on, Bobby began to develop habits that struck fear into Dorothy. She would come home and find him in white robes, perched regally on their white couch in a yoga position, using a golf club as a scepter. He wanted sketches of himself in this posture. All the women would gather on the floor while he shared "revelations" he had received about their innermost thoughts, even their dreams. The women were astonished and intimidated by his superhuman powers. But Dorothy wasn't surprised; Bobby had all of them keep diaries (he called them "growth journals"), and one of her wives-in-law was reading them and reporting their contents (even the terrible things that they thought and planned). For these revelations, they were physically punished.

One day, seated in kingly posture, he said, "I am the Word. The Word speaks through me. I am a vessel of the Word." He was beginning to presume a godlike authority to judge and punish the wrongdoings of the women. When his rules were broken, he would mete out the retribution. Some rules were not just personal, but generalized forbidden behavior, which all pimps try to enforce. A dictum such as "Never talk with other women about your man" discourages bad-mouthing and put-downs, while preventing women from comparing notes, which might create dissatisfaction and even anger. Some pimps must have feared the church bus because it provided opportunity for women to talk about their troubles in the household. During group conversations when a woman would begin (probably with good reason) to take off on her man, another would reprimand her, saying, "It's not right to talk about your nigger like that." (All the women referred to their men as niggers, and the term was not intended as a racial slur, nor did it indicate lack of love or respect.) But the rule probably was honored more in the breaking than in the keeping of it.

Bobby had always told Dorothy that if she ever wanted to leave the life, she should just tell him. So one day, gathering her courage, she told him she wanted to get out. Immediate violence: He got a .38 pistol and held it to her head. Pushing her against a sixteenth-floor balcony railing, he told her, "You and that life belong to me. If you don't want to do this, you must want to die." She begged for her life, and he let her off with a severe coat-hanger beating. Afterward, he announced he was moving out and never wanted to see her again, a promise he didn't mean to keep. He came back daily to talk with her, saying "her mind was all fucked up," she would never amount to anything. Dorothy said she would go back to work, but insisted that he never threaten her with a gun again.

Trying later to explain her irrational behavior, Dorothy saw herself as a masochist, feeling so unworthy that she had to stay in the life as punishment. What she said next helps explain why many women remain with abusive husbands. "If you are lonely for love, and you're not getting it, you'll settle for abuse. At least someone is paying attention to you." It is hard for an outsider to understand. Bobby hadn't slept with Dorothy for months; so much suffering and abuse without any sexual reciprocity! Yet she endured all this, for deeply ingrained in her was his belief that earthly pleasures were disgusting, only spiritual communion was true and good.

One day it came to Dorothy, just like one of Bobby's revelations, that she was a free woman. She knew that it was she herself that mattered; the man was nothing. She detested him —his lies, his phony posturings. That day she plotted to leave him and the life forever.

There were several false starts, but one night something so enraged him that he began to beat her. She knew he meant business when his fists began to strike her face, and she was terrified. A woman can be beaten on parts of her body that are not visible and she can continue working. A woman with a bruised face cannot make money, so Bobby obviously didn't care. It seemed as if he was going to kill her. Dorothy was in her nightgown and slippers, but the moment a chance came, she grabbed her trench coat and ran out of the apartment.

She arrived at the church at 10 P.M. Luckily, Howard was still in his office. He took Dorothy to Arlene's apartment in the church building, where she showered and borrowed some clothes. Then the two women headed to the emergency room at St. Vincent's Hospital, so that Dorothy's injuries could be treated.

When they returned to the church, Dorothy was so wound up that she spent the whole night talking. She couldn't believe what Bobby had done to her or what he had attempted to do. There was no turning back. After several days, Dorothy returned to her apartment at a time when she knew no one would be home, took some of "her" money from the stash Bobby kept hidden, and ran.

Bobby has never let her rest. Years later, he still calls constantly, tells her that she was and is the reason for his life. What he really means is that he realizes he had one of the brightest, most beautiful, highest-earning streetwalkers in New York. And he lost her forever to the self-knowledge and wisdom he encouraged her to seek.

Bobby doesn't sound like your typical pimp, but it became clear to us out on the street that the people seldom fit our images.

Gail was one of the first women we became deeply involved with. Lively and outspoken, she had been working about five years when she cornered us one night to ask help in regaining custody of her infant son. The police, looking for her man, had come to her hotel room seeking information. She may have known where Blue was, but was unwilling to tell the police his whereabouts. Whatever her reasons, they were infuriated, and declared that she would pay for her lack of cooperation. The following day her baby-sitter opened the door to find several police officers, who forced their way into the room and, without explanation, took Michael and left. Gail soon discovered that the boy had been placed with a foster family on Long Island.

Gail, beside herself, didn't know what to do. We didn't either, but we did know a young lawyer who we thought might be willing to help. Gail hired him. He learned that the police had removed her child illegally and began procedures to have him returned to Gail's custody. She was afraid that things would move too slowly. At the same time, the lawyer (whose wife had just given birth to their first child and who had a great deal of empathy) was offered, and accepted, a position out of the state. Under those circumstances, he and Gail decided that they should try to kidnap her child. Since the authorities had taken him away illegally, extreme measures for recovering him seemed well justified.

Gail had permission to visit Michael each week when his foster parents brought him for a medical exam at the New York Foundling Hospital. On one of those visits, Gail wrapped him in blankets and walked right out the door. Her lawyer remained behind, explaining to the authorities what she had done and why. The following day Gail, Blue, and Michael came to the church, and in a small private ceremony, Howard baptized the child. Afterward, they left New York for good.

Over the next couple of years the relationship between Gail and Blue deteriorated, and Gail left, taking Michael with her and refusing to tell Blue where they were living. But she kept in touch with us. A year later, we received a letter from Blue, asking us to help locate Gail and his son. It said, in part that he really missed his son, that it hurt every time he saw a little boy. He hadn't forgotten all the bad times that he put the two of them through. Yes, because "I tried so hard to get Gail to stay. I said I would help her in every way I could."

We let Gail know that Blue wanted to hear from her and eventually she made contact. From time to time she lets Michael visit him, and a relationship has developed between father and son.

While this experience informed our refusal to see all pimps as cut from the same cloth, we did have one encounter with a more stereotypical pimp. It took place when Fern came on board the bus in tears. Her man was looking for her because he'd heard that she was going to leave him. Word had come to her through the grapevine that he was going to "beat the shit out of that bitch." Although bigger and probably stronger than J.C., Fern was still terrified. She hated fights and tried to avoid them—and not only because she was afraid of getting hurt. Though on first meeting she appeared tough and dangerous, it soon became clear that she was a pussycat.

As she told her story, we could hear someone pounding on the outside of the bus and shouting words we couldn't understand. Howard rolled down the window of the driver's seat. J.C. came over, leaned inside, and said to Fern, "Bitch, you get out here *now*. You ain't leaving me till *I* say so." Fern cowered in the rear of the bus crying, while Howard tried to talk J.C. down. Yelling at Fern wouldn't get him what he wanted. It only made matters worse. J.C. said that while he didn't want to "disrespect a man of God," he had to "take care of business," and asked Howard to *force* Fern to leave the bus. Rolling up the window, Howard asked Fern what she wanted to do, making it clear that we would help, whatever her choice. Fern was adamant that she didn't want to leave. J.C. was enraged when Howard told him what Fern had said. He became even more enraged when he found out that we were going to take Fern with us, and began shouting insults and epithets. Without another word, Howard started the motor, and with J.C.'s voice ringing in our ears, drove Fern to a small hotel near Penn Station so she could catch an early train to another city.

We expected this incident to be interpreted as an anti-pimp

attitude, and that the women would be forbidden to come on the bus. We were wrong. Everyone who mentioned it agreed that J.C. was a crazy SOB. No one had any sympathy for him. Our luck had held.

When a prostitute chooses a man, it seems as if her decision is based on many of the superficial judgments and ambiguous feelings that govern any woman's choice of a man in the square world. Sometimes romantic love is an ingredient in this complex relationship, but it appears to be clearly tempered by other considerations. The prostitute knows, for example, that there will most likely be other women in this relationship; therefore how she feels about those other women is important. Though she probably won't live with them, the odds are good that she will work with them on the stroll. The fact that she accepts other women in her relationship to her man does not mean she is resigned to them; there is something in the back of her head, if not deep in her heart, that tells her that those other women can't hold up to the competition she presents. The expectation is that "the man" will be satisfied by her charm and he won't need the others. The seeds of romantic love in monogamous relationships are planted deep in prostitutes, who, for all the deviancy of their life-style, hold out for that ultimate goal. What they probably miscalculate about "the man" is that his self-conception is very complex, and one of the things he is not (for the time being, at least) is a monogamous husband or lover. Consequently his attitude toward and treatment of his women will be complicated by his seeing them as employees, clients, and patients, and even sometimes as property. If we like to believe that this attitude is medieval and is seen only in pimps, let us not forget that at the roots of Western romantic love, consummated in marriage, there is a proprietary feeling that borders on ownership. The pimp may not pretend to that kind of love, but feels he has a relationship built on a certain understanding and set of rules.

In addition to the attraction or love that the prostitute feels for the man she chooses, there are other ingredients in her choice. He is desirable because she believes that he will be a good provider who will give her the things she needs (housing, food) and the things she desires (nice clothes, jewelry, a fur coat); and that he will give her the ultimate gift—he will let her bear his child.

Sure, I give him my money. So do a lot of other women who work to help support a family. I don't ask him to give me something in return. I guess he gives me himself, which is a helluva lot more than anyone else ever gave me. Of course he's got other women, and I know them. They live somewhere else now and he lives with me. Sometimes I feel I'm getting old and when a new, young woman comes along I feel emotional female things. It's not really jealousy, because being in the business, I know men cheat on their wives. To me, a pimp is much more honest. He's not going to pretend he's just yours.

Also figuring in her choice is his attractiveness to others, his looks, his fine clothing, his ostentatious automobile (the symbol of his competence). In other words, his desirability to other women is considered a premium, just as it is in a man chosen by many square women.

It is also important to women that their men be intelligent. One evening we asked a group of women to a meeting at Arlene's apartment. Among the other invited guests were Margaret Taylor, a New York City Family Court judge, and Ira Glasser, executive director of the American Civil Liberties Union. We wanted to bring them all together so that others, besides ourselves, would have an opportunity to hear directly from those affected how prostitution laws are enforced and how that enforcement disrupts their lives. Tiny, one of the women who attended, came armed with voluminous notes and lawbooks. Her man had prepared her for the meeting, had tutored her for weeks in advance. He was not going to let such a chance pass without giving it all he could, and Tiny's questions were right to the point. Our square guests were astonished.

After the choice is made, the relationship begins, including, if the prostitute is serious and the man is worthy, a dowry of perhaps several thousand dollars. Time passes and the pedestal may start to crumble, hopes begin to fade, as he turns out to be unreliable; but there is a loyalty in these women that is not ordinary. In this world where a woman doesn't talk about her man in front of other women, things have to get pretty bad before that rule is broken. Behavior needs to border on the intolerable: forgetting her birthday, or expecting her to work on that day; wasting days shooting dope with a wife-in-law while the other woman is working twelve hours; getting her an apartment, then failing to sleep with her for weeks on end. The women's toleration level for being wronged by their men seems incredibly high.

Mella had been with Joe for three years. Bright, humorous, sharp-tongued, she complained regularly about Joe's forgetting her birthday or being short of cash at Christmas. But she remained with him and was fiercely loyal, always making excuses. But one night her depression was apparent. After the other women had left the bus, she told us how angry she was at Joe, who, despite promises, had again ignored her birthday. All she wanted was a color television, and for months he'd given assurances that she was going to get one. Instead, he told her that evening it would have to wait until there was more money. "That motha is gonna have to find himself another bitch to pay his bills. Or let *him* stand out here and sell his ass. Last week I gave him two thousand dollars and it all went up his nose [cocaine]. He's not getting any more money from me. I'm gone."

Time and again we heard stories that were hard to accept, and often Arlene would help the women bring their feelings to consciousness and their anger to expression. There seemed to be in the women a blind spot toward their men, when they were the recipients of the most insufferable psychological or even physical abuse. However, a few years ago, when the hidden shame of America's middle-class marital life came to light —the battered-wife syndrome—the prostitute's staying with her man in spite of his abusive manner didn't seem all that abnormal. Dorothy's words came back again: "you'll settle for abuse. At least someone is paying attention to you."

One indicator of the relationship between a prostitute and her man is the living arrangement. How they live together and where are important barometers of the pimp's feelings and methods of control.

The popular misconception about prostitutes' lives is that their work and their lives beyond their work are all mixed up together: The hooker has a house or an apartment to which she brings tricks for sex, or to which the pimp brings patrons he has solicited for her. Actually, arrangements are various, depending on her man's inclinations. Where there is a pimp and his woman, they ordinarily share an apartment from which she goes to work. Her man may drive her to her workplace, which can be in another borough or state. Many of the street women on Manhattan's West Side live across the river in New Jersey motels near one of the tunnels, while some women working on the East Side have apartments in Queens and Brooklyn. But their work is their work, and their home is their home.

When a man has more than one woman, each may have her own place, the man living separately from all of them, or rotating. Though extravagant, this can protect the man's freedom and autonomy; it also avoids the antagonisms and jealousy that surface when several women live together. What for the man may be an escape from demands and conflict may appear to the woman a reward for the hard work and money she is bringing in.

Yet another kind of living arrangement is the extended family environment, where a man has several women and children and they share a house and probably two cars. In this instance the wives-in-law are of necessity much closer and share responsibilities for the children and the household. The neighbors may not know what the women do, or not care. They work somewhere else and come home from work just like "normal" people.

J., his six women and five children share a house in Queens. The women are genuinely devoted to one another and treat all the children like their own. If one of them becomes pregnant, she stays home, caring for the kids. She takes them to school and doctors, plans outings to the circus—does all the things any mother with five youngsters would do. If no one is pregnant, J. runs the household. The women work together on the street, look out for one another, and are as loyal to each other as to J. They tell us that the arrangement succeeds because they are working toward a common goal: the establishment of a family business. This is not a pipe dream. J. has invested in several ventures which, while they failed, did involve the participation of his women every step of the way. They all trust that sometime in the future the right opportunity will come along and that it will enable them to leave the streets forever.

Though these living arrangements exemplify the variety of housing, most common is a hotel or motel room, near or far from the stroll. Conservatively, the cost of housing for the working woman is approximately three hundred dollars a week, and the man's rent may raise this even higher.

Someone has said there are a lot of would-be pimps out there but very few real pimps. One thing we can be sure of is that the real ones are those who have mastered the life and its means of control. It is important for us to understand the nature of that life. No matter how far we have come in the general society vis-à-vis the emancipation of women and their equality with men, in this subculture of prostitution the man is still king of the hill while the woman is a submissive servant, albeit for the most part a *willing* one. It is still the most male chauvinist, sexist occupation and life-style extant in our society. The pimp must keep order and decorum in this complicated, volatile, and sometimes dangerous work/play life, where existence is transacted on the knife's edge of criminality and a vast shadow world of illicit activity. He lives only a moment away from being exterminated by a friend for his money, betrayed by a jealous woman for neglect, framed by a bigoted cop he stood up to. So his ability to dominate the environment over which he presides is critical, and that's what probably separates a "simple pimp" from a pro.

In most illicit subcultures (drugs, gambling, etc.), the rules of the game, the mores of that group, are crucial. In the world of prostitution, the pimp is the chief purveyor and interpreter of the rules that determine the appropriate behavior for everyone in the life. It is an oral tradition we are talking about; but anyone in or near the life knows the rules that prevail over the world where men and women collaborate in the profession of prostitution.

The chief article of faith in the tradition is that in this life the man is the king—his is the power and the dominion over the woman or women. In no other place in American life is the chauvinism so up-front and unambiguous: to keep women down, subjugated and inferior. Now, this is implicit in many occupational cultures in this nation's life, but in prostitution it is blatantly explicit. The woman is taught her subservient place by hundreds of little rituals and commands: "Get the potato chips"; "Do the dishes"; "Put the kid to bed"; "Never contradict me"; "Never show me up in front of my friends"; "It's time to get down" (go to work); "When I talk, you listen."

Another way of maintaining dominion is through restraining one's sexual desires. As contrary as this idea may be to our perception of the pimp, it is not an insignificant weapon in the struggle for dominance. It is his game plan to reverse the old notion of the man chasing the woman for something she has, and when he is approached, show reluctance to give up what he has—his sexual power to satisfy. There is an old street saying, "A good pimp keeps his dick in his pocket," which means he doesn't give sex unless he's paid. The pimp is the prostitute par excellence, never giving sex without reward. If our experience on the street is a good indicator, a lot of pimps are homosexual or bisexual.

This conjecture is supported by a recent incident on the church bus. Several flushed and highly excited women came on board. They had a piece of hot gossip to share and couldn't wait. Without revealing names, they told of a co-worker who had arrived home earlier than usual the previous day. Walking into her bedroom, she found her man and a male friend engaging in sex. Unseen, she tiptoed out of the house, claiming she would never return. Everyone was both shocked and titillated. There was a lot of speculation about the identity of the people involved, and several women passionately claimed that if it had been their man they would have killed him "then and there." Blue Eyes, who had remained thoughtfully quiet during most of the discussion, finally said with conviction that "it wouldn't have been so bad" if the pimp had "chosen to go with a transvestite." Arlene asked her what difference that would have made, since two men would still be having sex. After a few moments Blue Eyes answered that "while the body would be the same, the face would be a woman's. And that's easier to deal with."

The pimp knows that sex is a highly ambiguous tool in his work—he can manipulate his women with it, but it also can become the source of jealousy and fighting in his household. The racial myth of the black man with the outrageous libido, highly oversexed and possessed of incredible powers, is shattered by the pimp who has everything under control and uses his sex as a means to larger ends.

The pimp plays a mental game as much as or more than a physical or sexual game. He seems particularly adept at comprehending the world of fantasy that plays such a major part in the life of prostitution. He knows that his world is a lot like Hollywood, with a tremendous amount of playacting, pretending, and role playing. He is smart enough to realize that almost everyone lives off fantasies and dreams of one kind or another. Prostitution is built on the fantasies of the trick, whose flights of fancy drive him to the prostitute; her sexual secrets and finesse promise to take him to heights of sensual climax he has never known. But prostitution is also built on the dreams and visions of the women, for whom this strange world of fast tracks and shortcuts is only a brief digression in the quest for the fantasies that most people entertain—a better life, the enjoyment of pleasures, the luxury of good things, and finally the middle-class dream of "home and hearth," with children.

The pimp seems to be solidly in control of the fantasy that is at the heart of the willingness of the woman to work, to face dangers, to suffer ignominy and be subservient. She believes in the dream of the condo in the Caribbean, the boutique in Boston, and the children by the man she loves, which will be the reward for her labors. The man maintains control by manipulating the myths, extending the timetable of their reality, modulating them to fit his needs, and always promising the moon. His Cadillac and his diamonds are simply small precursors of the Big Promise that seldom comes, but the man knows he can bank on her need to cherish the dream, at least as long as she is useful and able to work. Those of us who stand outside and judge her naïveté, or ignorance, or emotional sickness, need only to be reminded of the last time we lived off the promises of a commitment that never came, or pinned our lives on a vision that was unreachable.

The control by the pimp—mentally, physically, and emotionally—is at the heart of the method by which he keeps his women in line. In order to accomplish this feat, his street smarts must be augmented by strong self-discipline and trained foresight. The would-be pimp who lacks these traits will probably drown in drugs or his own ego. The real pimp is cool and in control.

Something should be said here about women without men—those who, through circumstances beyond their control or more often by choice, work without a pimp, or more correctly, a man to whom they relate and give their money. In the life, these women are known as "outlaws," which might imply that they are "bucking the system" or refusing to "play the game" according to the rules. We have observed a decided increase in the number of such women in the last eight years. The women's liberation movement surely plays some role in this. These women, we noticed, usually have strong egos and a rather fierce independence. Many times they are veterans who have chosen finally to go it alone after disillusionment and dissatisfaction with "their people." Such women are heard to say often "never again," but they don't always mean it.

One would think that the outlaw would have much more money, since all of it is hers and none of it goes to support anyone except her children. However, that isn't the case. The only explanation is that since she has no pimp who motivates her to work and she has no wives-in-law with whom she is in competition for the pimp's affection and approval, the drive to make money is missing.

Though she is not that much better off financially, the woman who is ready to be on her own may have compensations. Some outlaws will choose to replace their pimp with a woman. That grows out of the need for companionship, coupled with the utter rejection of any man other than the ones she must work with (tricks, cops). Lesbian relationships are not anything like the norm, but there are a number of prostitutes who choose another woman to fill emotional needs and provide a stable relationship.

When Cookie was in jail for an extended period, her man

never visited, or wrote, or sent money. Her three children were cared for by her own mother during this time, but her man made no contribution toward their support. Nor did he try to raise money to pay her fine and get her out of jail. Furious, she shared her feelings of disappointment with another woman prisoner, who became a source of strength and comfort. For the remainder of her stay in jail this new friendship grew in importance. She also learned that her new friend was a lesbian.

Finally released, Cookie was unable to forgive her man for his indifference and refused to go back to him. At the same time she found herself missing the friend, who still had several months to serve. One night Cookie visited on the bus and, blushing and giggling, confided that she thought she might be gay. It worried her that she didn't have the slightest notion of what that meant. What she did know was that men had always let her down and she was ready to find out whether a woman could meet her unfulfilled needs.

What are we to conclude about society's "archvillains"? Probably that they are not as bad as pictured and that there are as many different kinds of pimps as prostitutes. As stated in the *Report of the Committee on Homosexual Offenses and Prostitution* published in Great Britain in 1957, although the pimp is a coercive figure in a prostitute's life,

> he is the only person in the world towards whom she feels affection and sense of possession; he is usually her champion in disputes. He is deeply despised by the police and the public outside his trade, but he may be nevertheless the one humanizing element in the life of the woman on whom he lives.

Perhaps there is no other way to understand the commitment, loyalty, and long suffering that the prostitute endures for "my people." If the police came anywhere near understanding this strong symbiotic relationship, they would abolish the "pimp squad" as an exercise in futility and eradicate those senseless, and even ludicrous, appeals to prostitutes posted on precinct walls:

ATTENTION PROSTITUTES OF NEW YORK

Are you tired of:

Giving all your money to your pimp?
Getting beat or abused when you don't make your trap?
Living on $5.00 a day while your man snorts the stack up
    his nose?
Spending nights in jail?
Walking the stroll and want to make a clean break?

We can help you to help yourselves. We can contact your concerned parents or relatives at your request.

Act now before it's too late! Contact
Manhattan South Morals Division
PIMP SQUAD

6

Cops and Courts: The Enforcement of an Unenforceable Law

As the years go on, there are more bad sides to my job, but the good sides are the money and not working 9 to 5. As everyone else will agree, the bad side is the cops, going to jail, sorry-ass tricks, and Society.

—SHANNON

We had not been on the streets very long, observing the night life on the stroll, before we recognized that the two most important men in a working woman's life besides her man and the trick are the policeman and the judge. They represent, for the most part, the enemy, albeit a necessary evil in the scheme of things. To us, coming from another world and having another perspective, the cops and the courts stand for the order that society tries to wrest from the potential chaos always lurking in our midst.

These servants of the civil order are the enforcers, and we are all dependent on their doing their job and doing it well. But at times the task we give them to do is an impossible one—the enforcing of what appear to be impossible laws. And when that is done, we make visible all the blemishes on the body of law enforcement.

In our work with prostitutes we experienced the shame and improbity of our system of law as it is embodied in mere humans, cloaked in uniforms and robes. If in the telling of this story it becomes obvious that the emperor has no clothes and the law is a travesty, it will not necessarily be because we have a bad cast of characters. Rather, we have imposed on the system an intolerable burden that brings out the worst in the enforcement of law and the structure by which justice is fairly and humanely dispensed.

Our first contact with law enforcement occurred a short time before Arlene and her colleagues from the church started their street contact with the women. Howard decided to be in touch with personnel at the Manhattan North precinct house who were responsible for dealing with prostitutes. It is the vice squad that is charged with the task of keeping the streets of Times Square safe from hookers and their pimps. On a bleak and windy night in March, Howard entered that seedy, run-down headquarters on Fifty-fourth Street near Eighth Avenue. As he encountered the noise and bedlam inside, he was amazed at how much it resembled all those police stations on TV dramas. Although it was early evening, the women were there in their working dress. One of them, large and black, was protesting loudly in language easily recognizable to any ex-marine. She yelled ever so indelicately that the animal who ran her in was a lying SOB when he said she was soliciting, because she was on her way to the store to buy groceries. It was a protest we would witness many times in the future, but it sounded then like one more person in custody protesting innocence.

Howard hurried by the bedlam to another room to ask for the officer in charge of the vice squad, and was introduced to the lieutenant. A slender man with a narrow face, he was graying at the temples, and seemed like a decent and ordinary person. Identifying himself, Howard explained that our church was contemplating doing work with the women. That guarded look common to every precinct officer when a civilian enters the station house disappeared and his face was pleasant. He spoke of the tragedy of the women and how unfortunate it was that the police had to arrest them. He sounded genuinely sympathetic as he mentioned his own young daughter and how he felt for these young women forced into such a terrible life. He was all for the church trying to help them out of the life. How many times we were to hear that welcome in the years to come! Howard didn't try to explain our mission differently as the officer went on to warn that the pimps would probably make our work very difficult, but he admired our willingness to try and help these "poor, unfortunate girls." Having been assured that the police were sympathetic to prostitutes, Howard walked back through the booking room, where a group, handcuffed and chained together, was being cursed, shoved around, and treated like hardened, dangerous criminals. As he left the building, Howard tried to reconcile the lieutenant's words with what he had seen.

It wasn't long before we learned that the attitudes and actions of the police fit no logic. They are indicative of a wrenching ambivalence, fed by a deep resentment toward the women who cause the public to put them, the cops, in the despicable role of moral wet nurses to a society for whom "immorality" is a way of life. We were to discover in our work just how outrageously ambiguous the role of the police is in trying to confine, curtail, and abolish a "commerce" that the makers of the law want to repudiate and punish but not really to destroy.

It doesn't take too much reasoning to understand that the police are handmaidens of lawmakers and public officials, whose task it is to tend, control, and keep order in the streets and public places. One must remember that fundamentally the police take their orders from a higher place. This doesn't mean that there aren't occasions when police act in a quasi-judicial manner by selectively enforcing particular statutes in order to restrain certain social behavior, but for the most part the police are *used* by politicians and the public. No matter how angry we may get at the behavior of policemen and the abuse of their power, they are finally manipulated and protected by public officials and laws. This disclaimer in no way cancels officers' responsibility for their acts and behavior, but it is important to put our experiences and the prostitutes' daily contacts with policemen in a larger context.

We were soon to learn that the street is a large stage upon

which a very old melodrama takes place every day and night. In this drama the two major characters are the prostitutes and the police—their parts are written and their movements directed by public and political pressures. The "sporadic clean-ups" and "media concentrations" are simply occasional ballyhoos for the real show, which does not change one scene in the long-running drama of the streets. The women know both their parts and their places very well and they are relatively uncomplicated. The role of the police is much more complex and depends on many factors. Society has made that role into one which requires a very special actor. The following telling description of a policeman by an Englishman gives us some clues to our protagonist.

> The true copper's dominant characteristic if the truth be known is not those daring or vicious qualities that are sometimes attributed to him by friend or enemy, but ingrained conservatism and a desperate love of the conventional. It is untidiness, disorder, that a copper disapproves of most of all, far more even than a crime, which is merely a professional matter. Hence his profound dislike of people loitering in the streets, dressing deviantly, speaking with exotic accents, being strange, weak, eccentric or simply any rare minority— of their doing anything in fact that cannot be safely predicted. (Colin McInnes, *Mr. Love and Justice* [London, 1962])

This seems to be an accurate description of the average policeman anywhere. Accepting it, one can discern quickly the antagonisms that feed the nightly melodrama. As the legislators try increasingly to determine social conduct and label moral crimes, the greater is the temptation for the police to develop an attitude toward a criminal class. If policemen already have a tendency to seek out deviation from normality in the execution of their duty, then more rigorous definition of that "normality" will encourage cops to treat all types of deviant behavior as criminality. When you add to this a public outcry for getting rid of a disreputable class, then you have all the makings of a crusade, with obvious violations of people's civil liberties.

Systematic harassment of prostitutes becomes a method of control even if the prostitute is not working, which is clearly a violation of her rights.

Another consequence of this legal moralism (making the police enforcers of social conduct) is to encourage the police toward abuse of their power, because it criminalizes the whole environment. Once police surveillance is moved beyond crimes of assault on people or property, you make the work appear more dangerous. The more the cop's daily task is to observe deviations from the norm, the more suspicious he becomes of any aberrant behavior on the street, whether it endangers anyone or not. The prostitute is one among many such "deviants," and there is a long history (at least a hundred years) of symbiotic relations between police and prostitutes in this country.

One of the factors that make the relationship so difficult for the prostitute is the enforcer's ambivalence. That translates into a kind of Jekyll-Hyde mentality where, on the one hand, the cop plays the role of a militant reformer crusading against these "despicable criminals" who threaten him and everyone else on the street, and on the other, he propositions his favorite prostitute to service all the policemen at a bachelor party.

> *You know that fuzz got some gall. He saw me down at 100 Centre. I just got out of court after forty-eight hours in the pit, and he says come on, I want to show you something. He takes me to some kind of policeman's room and he says he wants a blow job. I can't believe that man. He's one who is always picking on us. He says to me, "You owe me one. I let you go one night when I shoulda hauled your ass in." I didn't want no trouble, so I gave him the blow job right there on top of the desk. I bet that motha didn't write that one up. Can you believe that?*

If we have some illusion that the police are different from the average male population and because of their job don't need or use prostitutes, we need to reassess our stereotypes. They are no better and no worse; it's just that their hypocrisy is a little more repulsive.

As in any symbiotic relation, the two parties live off each other in a mutually acceptable manner. The prostitute knows that the cop on the vice squad has a job to do—to "catch a case," and she is the case he is trying to catch. They are playing a street game, and the game has its rules. The prostitute knows that if the cop catches her fair and square while she is soliciting him, and she hasn't been to jail for a while, then she won't resent the arrest. The police know the prostitute is going to be on the street every night and she will try to elude him. A police lieutenant describes the game:

> We're only assigned [to the vice squad] for two months because the girls get to know who we are. As soon as they recognize us we've outlived our usefulness. . . . You do have to be a little bit of an actor. One officer walked around with a cast on his leg, another with crutches. The guys go out with briefcases and glasses—so you're just another man. But the girls are very street wise. They know cops. They're like bird dogs. They'll search you, pick up your pants to look for an ankle holster. They'll actually fondle you, looking for your gun.

It's all part of the game, with two sides and unwritten rules. As with any play between the powerful and the powerless, those who initiate the game make and break the rules. We could never understand the women's apparent benevolence toward the police, when there are constant stories of physical abuse, false arrests, etc. But in time, we learned that the women accept the "illegality" of their own activity, and therefore expect the police to view them the same way and treat them accordingly.

To illustrate how mutual is the game, the policeman believes that when he tells a woman to get out of his precinct because the pressure's on to clean up the street, or when he has his nightly quota to meet and picks a woman for arrest at an appointed time and place and tells her to be there, compliance is in order. The arresting officer has control over the actions of the prostitute. Whether she is brought into the precinct house handcuffed, screaming, and cursing the world, or whether she is fairly docile, resigned, and even joking, is very much in the hands of the police. If the cop in a legitimate arrest goes out of his way to degrade the prostitute, treating her cruelly as an object of public contempt and derision rather than as a working woman doing her job, then he calls forth from her a negative and harsh reaction. The game and the woman's role as adversary to the cop's protagonist is accepted by prostitutes, but when the cop fails to abide by the rules and becomes some other character, who treats her in an inhumane manner, then the woman is incensed and turns on him.

Now, a sassy prostitute, like an "uppity nigger" in Southern culture, is a threat to the power and dominion of the police. She's an affront to the policeman's competence and ability as an officer—that is, his superiority and authority over the person being arrested. To challenge his arrest (if he is not playing the rules) or to react in kind to his unnecessary put-down of her moral character undermines his position as the one in control. The relationship of police and prostitute, as distinct from other criminals, is patterned and predictable.

For example, when there are no pressures and the status quo is being maintained, the "beatwalker" may treat women on the stroll just like any other members of the neighborhood—sometimes friendly chats, other times information passed, even help given, in hot pursuit of a criminal. There is a live-and-let-live air at times which lulls the women into letting their guard down.

Another interesting relationship between police and prostitute on the street grows out of common interests: A special detail of police is assigned to potentially high-crime areas such as Times Square and the Port Authority Bus Terminal, plainclothesmen in unmarked cars whose task it is to spot criminal activity in progress and intercept it; all street crime except prostitution is under their surveillance. The women on the street are always relieved to see that an unmarked car is not the vice squad but anticrime, preparing for a "sweep." The women are friendly with anticrime officers and at times give them valuable information that assists in the apprehension of criminals. For example, during the summer months there is gang activity that is a form of street hustle wherein several teenage boys surround a pedestrian, bump into him, lift his wallet, and then in the noise and confusion disappear around a corner. These late-night marauders drive off potential clients and are anathema to prostitutes, who feel no compunction about cooperating with anticrime efforts to arrest these criminals. An interesting aspect of this behavior is its indication that despite the strong predisposition of the law to drive the prostitute into protective collusion with street criminals, there are certain crimes that the women find odious, even as middle-class victims do. This is not high morality in action. Some of the women would see nothing wrong in lifting money from a drunken trick —but only if there was an excessive amount of money, if the trick was overtly careless about it, and if she thought there was a good chance she could get away with it.

An ethicist would be hard-pressed to distinguish the fine lines the prostitute draws on these matters, but fundamentally she rationalizes that the intimacy she has shared (voluntarily) and the service she has rendered entitle her to take more if the opportunity arises. This is particularly true if the client is "stupid enough" to carry large amounts of money into such a precarious and potentially dangerous place with a complete stranger. The temptation is great and the human will is weak, which is why anticrime occasionally engages in entrapment procedures. The ruse is to put a supposedly sleeping drunk on the street as a decoy, with money sticking out of his pocket, to play upon that human weakness. This game is not apt to snare streetwise hustlers, who recognize the ploy; it will be more likely to entrap a poor innocent who has never stolen anything before. At any rate, in spite of the fact that prostitutes are criminals in the eyes of the law, there is a certain camaraderie among anticrime cops and the women, due to a common concern for street safety.

The police of the vice squad, however, are another matter for prostitutes, and the symbiosis there results in each having almost stereotypical expectations of the other. Prior to 1976, the only weapon the police had against streetwalkers was arrest for direct solicitation, and the courts held the police accountable for following protocol. Women look back to this period as the time of the fair fight. If the police in pursuit of their duty could catch them unaware, however difficult going to jail might be, somehow the system gave them a break. If the women were smart and experienced enough, they could elude all the ploys of entrapment. Even in this more idyllic world of adversarial positions, when the police lied about the facts the prostitutes had no equity in the situation. Judge John Murtagh, who back in those days was the chief magistrate in Women's Court and heard many cases, comments:

> How can there be a fair trial on so important a case when it is repeatedly reduced to a question of veracity between an accused person and a police officer? If you were a judge would you find it easy to call a guardian of the law a liar? And so it is that while in other courts defendants are presumed innocent until proved guilty, here it seems to be the other way around. (*Cast the First Stone* [Greenwood Press, 1978], p. 257)

It is an irony that in a period when prostitutes felt they got an even break from the police, the system really presumed them guilty if it was their word against a cop's. What they probably perceived "as a better time" in their work world was dependent somewhat on the police and the prostitutes' not lying but playing the game fairly.

Another example of playing the game fairly was that the police would not use unnecessary force. This rule was highly unreliable because of individual policemen with excessive animosity toward the working women, which came out in the form of needless brutality. One of the most infamous cops on the beat was known as "Crazy Beast." There are countless stories about the night when Crazy Beast "went off " on them. Physical abuse was his way of dealing with the women, and there was never any desire on their part to develop cordial relations. It is clear that what he wanted was that the very sight of him evoke terror in the streetwalkers. He got that, along with a lot of enmity and loathing. However, when street criminals gunned him down one day on the corner of Forty-second Street and Eighth Avenue, the women, despite all the misery and abuse he had visited on them, said they felt sorry for him and wouldn't have wished such an end for him. Crazy Beast, critically injured, survived and was later assigned to a desk job.

One of the questions about police brutality toward prostitutes is whether it is elicited because the prostitutes don't respect the policeman's authority. When he tells them to get lost, and they don't, he has to show them. After all, the women, whom he usually knows well, are not playing their part when, for example, they run away as he tries to arrest them to fill his quota. So when he catches them, he manhandles them, pulling their hair, banging their heads against buildings, and on occasions, in a frenzy of humiliation, using his club. When a woman protests, he will reply, "You shouldn't have run from me"—that is, the abuse is punishment for not "playing your part." On the other hand, the woman feels that going to jail is punishment for failing to elude the cop in the chase. The policeman's justification is that "she should have known better; I've told her if she ever ran and I caught her I'd bust her head."

There is no justification for the treatment that Susan Heeger, a nonprostitute, received at the hands of a vice squad cop on the night of July 20, 1978, at Lexington Avenue and Twenty-eighth Street. Here are the words of an eyewitness:

> Immediately after I saw her I saw an American car screech to a halt near her and a man in a T-shirt jump out and grab Heeger by her hair. He flung her to the sidewalk by her hair and kneeled down

with his knees in her stomach. Heeger started screaming hysterically for help and for someone to call the police . . . then the man began to drag Heeger by the hair across the street, from time to time kneeling on her stomach. She kept screaming help, someone call the police!

Only later did she realize the terrifying truth: The man assaulting her *was* the police. And further, she received the treatment because Officer Constantino of Midtown South thought she was a prostitute. Obviously, if he had known she was a Harvard-educated editor working at St. Martin's Press, he would have treated her differently.

It is this kind of violence that prostitutes consider a gross violation of the rules of the game and their rights as human beings. We are not contending that all cops treat streetwalkers like this, but we suggest that verbal and physical abuse are not isolated incidents in the enforcement of antiprostitution laws.

Then there are policemen like Officer X, a black officer who would join the foot chase after women but never catch them, not because he couldn't but because he didn't want to. He treated the women with respect and as equals. Sometimes he would warn them when a particularly antagonistic cop was on the warpath and would be picking up between midnight and 2 A.M. His generosity and deference endeared him to the women, and when he had to make an arrest there was no resentment. He was a fair player in those complex night games.

One of the turning points in the relationship between law enforcement and the prostitutes came in 1976 with the McCall-Ohrenstein loitering law. New York Penal Law 240.37 was partly a preparation for the Democratic National Convention and partly a more effective weapon for arrest and incarceration of the women. It was the law that Arlene's class-action suit sought to declare unconstitutional. The new law certainly furnished the police with a large broom with which to clean the streets, but intended as an effective police weapon that would protect certain civil liberties at the same time, it helped neither because of its vagueness and its prerequisites to arrest.

For example, the woman to be arrested had to be seen beckoning, gesturing, and repeatedly attempting to communicate with males in a proscribed public area. After Arlene's arrest, we became much more observant of police action on the street. We wanted to see whether there was any real compliance with the prerequisites of the loitering act. It was our observation that more often than not, the police violated the arresting codes of the statute. The fact was that even with this new law, which gave them a much easier instrument for arresting prostitutes, police were still unable to avoid "illegal arrests."

Now look at the symbiotic relationship again. The police had acquired, by virtue of their power to change the rules of the game, a new law that made the prostitute much more vulnerable to arrest and gave the police a distinct advantage. But even with this new law, which the women became resigned to, the police could not comply with requirements that had been written for their distinct benefit. There is no more serious threat to the rights of everyone in a society than illegal arrests, a form of abuse of power made more intolerable because it is used by law enforcement officers who already have considerable power.

The problem with using a poorly written law to ensnare prostitutes is that it places the police in the position of having to abuse the power of law. Society may not care, as long as it is an effective tool against prostitutes because of their "undesirable" status, but either an unenforced law or a law whose legal protections cannot be observed will encourage in both prostitutes and police a disrespect for the law in general.

How else can one understand some of the new games the police are playing? Women had always told us that police officers in squad cars driving through the Times Square area carried books in which the names of all the working women were listed. They also contained the dates on which the women were scheduled for their next arrest! Often women would be told a day or two in advance to "make your money because you're going [to jail] on Wednesday." We were somewhat skeptical of these reports, while not entirely doubting them. However, in the summer of 1984, while speaking at a Manhattan precinct, we were assured by several police officers that they indeed did carry such a book in their squad car, always had done so, and believed that officers elsewhere did the same thing.

However, when the crackdown on Eighth Avenue came in the late seventies, many of the women moved to an area from Thirty-seventh to Forty-second streets between Eleventh and Twelfth avenues. It was territory considered dangerous by many Times Square prostitutes, who said they would never work there, but necessity has modified their fears and many work there now. It is surrounded by warehouses and bus parking lots, and is devoid of normal pedestrian traffic. The clients are all "car tricks," the streets in this area being entrances and exits to the Lincoln Tunnel. The major concentration of the women is a particularly long and ominous block, Thirty-ninth between Eleventh and Twelfth. There are as many as thirty prostitutes working there round the clock, sometimes undisturbed but at other times harassed and chased and rounded up.

It was in this area, because of its isolation, lack of public scrutiny, and the aggregation of women, that the police engaged in some of their most malevolent behavior. It began with petty acts of harassment, such as grabbing women's wigs off their heads and confiscating them so that they couldn't work anymore, stealing their shoes to put an end to their walking the streets. (For some women, wigs are a disguise which protect them from recognition by acquaintances who are unaware of their work; for others, the wig establishes their attractiveness, so that tricks may be more likely to seek their services.) These affronts were offensive enough in their contempt, but they got worse when officers played games to see who was going to be arrested at a given time. The street was easy to block off, and they would line up white prostitutes on one side of the street and blacks and Hispanics on the other. They would then command a foot race from one end of the street to the other, with the losing group to be jailed. Besides being offended by the brutish sexism and racism inherent in that act, we ought to take umbrage at the arbitrariness and injustice with which the law is enforced.

Another competitive game the police played with the women might be called a "trick tournament," in which the women were pitted against each other to see who could get tricks in a given time period. Those who had not succeeded would have to go to jail! Where in our society could law enforcement officers act in such callous disregard of citizens' rights, except among these women outcasts? When officers act in this manner, the law is dishonored and disparagement of the police is encouraged.

We need to reiterate that not all policemen are guilty of this kind of behavior. And we have discovered that there are increasing numbers of officers who believe the law should be changed. They are aware that in the scale of crimes that matter, solicitation for the purposes of prostitution has a low claim on the time and energy of law enforcers.

Let us turn now to that other aspect of the enforcers, the judges and their courts. It should come as no surprise that the locale where justice is bestowed is by its nature reflective of the mediocre and somewhat dismal quality of the way our system of jurisprudence works.

Manhattan's Criminal Court Building at 100 Centre Street is a run-down, dingy, dreary structure, where prostitutes are arraigned twenty-four hours a day. The hallways are always filled with men and women, young and old, trying—often without success—to locate the courtroom where a friend or relative will be brought for arraignment. Nothing has been done to make the search easy. Information is scarce and, when available, rudely delivered; lists of names and docket numbers which should be posted in advance of court appearances more often than not are Scotch-taped to the marble walls hours after the person has been arraigned; and the atmosphere is tense as people wander in and out of courtrooms looking for their loved ones, complaining about the length of time they have been waiting. No chairs or benches furnish the hallways; people can be found sitting or dozing on the dirty marble floors, some eating sandwiches brought from home (especially in the evening, when the only coffee shop in the courthouse is closed). Children of all ages accompany their parents, and baby carriages and strollers add to the air of confusion.

The daily cast of characters includes police officers, who are everywhere, one for each case to be arraigned. Out of uniform, they are easily identified, and it is surprising how much they resemble one another. Male and female officers share a similar going-to-court uniform: jeans, T-shirts, and the ever-present shield dangling from their belts or clipped to the neck of their jerseys. They behave as though the courtroom were their private clubhouse, sitting and chatting among themselves as they wait for their case to be called. Only once in a while does a court officer or judge ask them to be quiet.

Private attorneys are always present; identified by their suits and briefcases, they are, for the most part, white males. Some are regulars who hang around the courtroom twelve to fourteen hours a day picking up "on the spot" business from pimps, prostitutes, and drug dealers, from whom they get their fifty-dollar fee up front. Others have been called there by distraught families they have never met to represent clients they have never seen. They stride confidently through the courtroom calling the family's name, and sit with them long enough for the three-hundred- to five-hundred-dollar cash fee to be handed over. And then there are the Legal Aid lawyers, a mixed bag of men and women of all ages, who will represent anyone without the funds to hire private counsel.

Another segment of the courtroom population consists of the court officers, spiffy in starched uniforms, with highly visible guns in holsters riding on their hips. Some are officious, others pleasant, but all are intimidating as they stand at their posts watching the audience, making sure that no one talks to a neighbor, reads a newspaper, eats a candy bar, or motions or signals to a prisoner on the bench. They work in tandem with the clerical staff that handles the paperwork for each case while court is in session.

Then there are the judges: male and female, black and white, youthful and elderly. Some appear interested in the cases before them, others are indifferent; some are rude to prisoners, others polite; some are punctual, others chronically late; some pontificate from the bench, others keep their feelings to themselves and do their job.

Last but not least are the prisoners, without whom everyone else would be seeking employment elsewhere. They sit crowded together on the benches where a jury would normally be seated. Often there are so many bodies crammed into a small space that only a portion of a prisoner's rear end actually rests on the seat. Largely male, the majority black or Hispanic, they look tired, disheveled, and often surly. How many days they have been in jail awaiting arraignment is unknown.

Arraignments take place in two courtrooms that formerly served as Manhattan's traffic court. They look like any other courtroom, except that there is no witness stand; instead a rectangular table sits on the floor below the bench and everyone —prisoner, arresting officer, counsel to the defendant, and prosecutor from the district attorney's office—stands facing the judge. What the audience sees is a picture of great confusion, with as many as twenty-five people walking and talking around the judge's platform while a case is being heard. Unless the judge makes an effort, and few ever do, the audience is unlikely to hear what is happening with a particular prisoner. Evidently this is of no concern to anyone in the courtroom except the prisoner's family.

The arraignment procedure is simple and straightforward. In

theory, everyone arrested in Manhattan will be arraigned within twenty-four hours. In practice, it almost always takes longer, sometimes up to three or four days. This important first step in the legal process gives prisoners an opportunity to proclaim their innocence or admit their guilt to charges brought against them. The arresting officer is present to swear to the charges, and if the prisoner pleads guilty the judge imposes sentence on the spot; no trial will take place. If the prisoner pleads not guilty, a trial date is set and, at the discretion of the judge, the prisoner is either returned to prison to await trial, or released on bail or on his own recognizance.

Where prostitution arrests are concerned, the arraignment procedure was recently changed, and the difference is significant. Unlike other prisoners, prostitutes are *prearraigned* before they are taken to court. What that means is that immediately after arrest, a prostitute is removed to Central Booking, where the arresting officer swears out a deposition describing the circumstances under which she was taken into custody. The truthfulness of that deposition is sworn to in court by another police officer, who acts as a stand-in for all prostitution cases on a given shift. In other words, prostitutes do not face their accusers in the initial stage of the judicial process. The rationale for this change in policy was to reduce the length of time police officers spend in court and save the department money ordinarily used for overtime. The unspoken assumption on which the policy is built is that prostitutes always plead guilty, and therefore it is a waste of the department's time to have dozens of officers sitting in court waiting to appear before the judge.

We were drawn into this aspect of prostitutes' lives in 1981 when word came that a woman we knew had been badly beaten and arrested on Eleventh Avenue. Concerned for Cheri's safety, we were asked by some of her friends to go to court and be there for her. We sat in the courtroom for three consecutive days, waiting while other women, some of whom had been arrested a day or two after Cheri, were arraigned. We were told by women we knew that she was in the holding pen downstairs, but no one could explain why her arraignment was being delayed. Then, on the morning of the fourth day, Cheri was escorted into the courtroom, pale and obviously angry, her hair and clothes rumpled. She sat on the bench throughout the morning session waiting for her case to be called, while dozens of other prisoners were brought into the room and appeared before the judge. Finally, in the middle of the afternoon, it was her turn to be arraigned; she pleaded guilty to loitering, was sentenced to a two-hundred-dollar fine, given a month to raise the money, and released.

Afterward, over hamburgers, Cheri told the story of her arrest. She had just arrived at Eleventh Avenue, ready to start work, when a squad car pulled up and ordered her inside. The police did not need to tell her that she was under arrest for loitering. A veteran of thirteen years in the business, Cheri was unwilling to automatically assent to what she considered a less than "righteous" arrest, so she argued with the officers and refused to go with them. That's when they roughed her up and carted her off to jail. Cheri was furious and let it be known at the police station that she was going to plead not guilty at arraignment. The police retaliated by tacking onto the loitering charge the more serious charge of resisting arrest.

Three days in jail weakened her resolve to plead not guilty. There was no denying who had the upper hand and what the outcome was likely to be. After all, as each day passed it was unmistakably clear that the police were preventing her arraignment and would continue to do so until she gave in. With a four-year-old daughter at home and bills to pay, her priority was to get out of jail. She could foresee that the consequences of standing up for her rights might mean being held over for trial at Rikers Island.

So a deal was struck between Cheri and the police: She would plead guilty to loitering; in exchange they would drop the charge of resisting arrest. And that's exactly what happened. No consultation with lawyers; Cheri negotiated directly with the police and was "persuaded" that pleading guilty was in her best interests.

Who could argue with her decision? She had no desire to be a martyr and didn't believe that our judicial system was designed to protect her rights. After three days in jail she would have done or said anything to get out.

Cheri's story and our own courtroom observations during that time raised a multitude of questions about how prostitutes are treated by our legal system and led us to begin a weekly vigil at 100 Centre Street in the hopes of finding some answers.

Over time, we recognized another reason for being there: It was for the women, those we already knew and others we would meet at the courthouse. Rarely is there a friendly or sympathetic face awaiting a prostitute entering arraignment court. (Contrary to popular mythology, pimps rarely arrange to get their women out of jail. The women are expected to work out that problem—like all others—on their own.) In an environment that is hostile, our presence seemed to matter. We would carry a bunch of coins for phone calls, subway tokens, and always lots of cigarettes. Smiles came to the women's faces when they saw us, and they would stop for a few moments of whispered conversation despite their desire to get going. Often, out on the bus the night after a day in court, women would mention that they had heard through the grapevine that we had been at Centre Street. And as time passed, if we missed our regular court day we would get complaints from women who had been arraigned. We became convinced that being there for them was an important component of our ministry.

To establish ourselves as a legitimate presence in the court environment, we wore name tags that identified us as part of the Judson Church Prostitution Project. These aroused the curiosity of lawyers, police, court personnel, pimps, prostitutes, and visitors as well, enabling us to make contact quickly and develop relationships that were both helpful and informative. In time, this led to introductions to judges who learned of our presence. We would be called into chambers by a judge who was interested in learning more about our work; or we would request permission through friendly court personnel to speak with a judge about a whole range of issues related to prostitution.

A new mythology developed among the women, who came to believe that judges were somehow more lenient when we were present in court. This was probably not true, but when you are as powerless as those women are, you're inclined to grasp at any magical explanation of why the system is treating you kindly.

Recently, a judge who had eight women awaiting arraignment on prostitution charges asked us to come into his chambers during recess. When court resumed, every woman coming before him was given Time Served; not only on the immediate charge but for outstanding warrants as well. (Time Served means that the time a woman has been held in custody awaiting arraignment is considered by the judge to be her sentence.) The women, stunned and delighted by his generosity, attributed it all to our presence. Given who the judge was, the interpretation is unlikely, but that event is what mythology is built on.

A typical day in arraignment court would begin at about 9:30 A.M., when prisoners would be brought into the courtroom and seated on the bench—unless, in the lingo of the court, "leftovers" from the previous shift were already there. Males would have been seen by their attorneys in private interview rooms adjacent to the court. Female prisoners are not shown the same courtesy. Interviewed by counsel in the courtroom within hearing of other prisoners, they are inhibited from sharing confidences with their lawyers.

This lack of privacy may also contribute to the refusal or unwillingness of most prostitutes to plead not guilty when they believe themselves to have been falsely arrested. It would take more than just a hurried courtroom conversation to persuade a woman with an extensive arrest record that she has the right to protest her innocence and that to do so would not necessarily result in the setting of high bail, causing her to remain in custody until trial.

The absence of privacy for lawyer and female client is made dramatically clear when a woman with no prior arrest record pleads guilty to a charge of prostitution. Even the most punitive of judges will raise a question with the attorney about whether the prisoner understands the meaning of the plea, indicating that judicial leniency would be granted a prostitute on her first arrest. When that occurs, the lawyer will usually explain the alternatives to the prisoner—something that ought to have happened before the case was called. There have been times, perhaps because the woman did not fully understand her options, when she refused to change her plea to not guilty. Were there ample opportunity for lawyer and client to meet under less stressful and public circumstances, it is hard to imagine that any woman would choose a two-hundred-dollar fine over the dismissal of charges.

For some years, there have been promises—as yet unfulfilled —that women's interview facilities would be created by the court. Whether that will ever happen is moot.

Ordinarily, when a group of male prisoners is brought into arraignment court, they are people who have been charged with a variety of crimes: shoplifting, drug dealing, car theft, assault, etc. Prostitutes, on the other hand, are brought into court as a class, eight or ten at a time. Compounding that cruel reality is the length of time they wait to be called before the judge, as compared to male prisoners. More often than not they will sit on the bench from early morning till midafternoon, while twenty-five or thirty male prisoners enter and are arraigned ahead of them. The women, some scantily dressed, are left vulnerable, sitting for hours in full view of the audience. Once in a while a policeman or court officer will snicker, point at a particular woman, and ridicule her appearance, and when the judge or the lawyers realize what is happening, they may join in the "fun."

Occasionally a woman will signal that she needs to use a bathroom, hoping to catch the attention of an officer. Court personnel are either blind or indifferent (we suspect the latter), and it may take half an hour before someone pays attention and meets her request. One can easily imagine the humiliation of being put on display and held up to public derision for hours at a time, deprived of privacy or protection. It appears to be a deliberate way of further humiliating and punishing prostitutes, since there exists no logical reason to bring them into the courtroom if they are not ready to be arraigned.

When prostitution cases are finally called, sentencing is invariably the same for all women appearing before a particular judge. Prior arrest records or the circumstances of the arrest make no difference; most judges have usually decided in advance what sentence will be meted out for this misdemeanor.

One of the more hypocritical aspects of the sentencing of prostitutes occurs when they are fined and given time to come up with the necessary cash. The way it works is this: The judge will sentence a woman to a two-hundred-dollar fine or ten days in jail. He will then ask the woman's attorney how much time she will need to get the money together. Usually a month is requested, and a date is set for the woman to return to court to pay her fine. Everyone—the judge, the lawyers, the police, the woman herself—realizes that the only way she can hope to raise the money is by going right back out on the street and prostituting herself. Nevertheless the charade continues, and the public is persuaded that prostitution is discouraged by arrests. A case could be made that it is instead perpetuated by legal sanctions which cause women to work longer and harder to make the money with which to pay their fines.

When society complains about the existence of street prostitution, it is unaware that the enforcement of our existing laws results in an increase, rather than a decrease, in the length of time women spend soliciting on the streets. Someone who might normally work an eight- or ten-hour shift may extend that to fifteen hours to pay her fines. Bear in mind that most Manhattan prostitutes are arrested once or twice a week, and you will have a good picture of just how our system contributes to the "problem" of street prostitution.

In 1983, the hours Manhattan's arraignment court was kept open and functioning were extended round the clock. This was in response to criticism of the length of time it was taking to arraign most prisoners, often two and three days. That the new hours made not a whit of difference in cases of prostitution comes as no surprise. In fact, their waiting time often increased.

The indifference of the court was demonstrated one day when we arrived at 9:30 A.M. to find eight women sitting on the bench waiting to be arraigned. The lawyers and all court personnel were there, ready for the day's shift to begin. But a key person was missing: the judge. A capacity audience waited with growing impatience as ten o'clock, eleven o'clock, and then noon came and went without the arrival of the judge. No explanation was offered, and the circumstances were so outrageous that we decided to intervene. Crossing the corridor to another arraignment court, which was in recess, we managed to speak with the judge. He seemed genuinely shocked that prisoners had been left to sit on the bench for that length of time, and offered to find out what was going on. After a brief telephone conversation, he explained that the judge who had been due to sit on the bench that day was testifying at the trial of a colleague. However, he was expected in court sometime after lunch. That meant not before two o'clock, a wait of five hours for the women. Protesting the unfairness of this situation, we asked whether the prisoners might be brought into his court for arraignment. Taken aback by our suggestion, he explained that it was impossible because the logistics of the building prevented the movement of prisoners from one courtroom to another. However, he volunteered that "If Judge _____ isn't here by one o'clock, I'll go over there and arraign the women myself."

Moments before the one o'clock lunch break, the tardy judge arrived, yet we were convinced that had we not intervened, and had he been delayed until three or four in the afternoon, no one would have made an effort to protect the interests of the women prisoners or been concerned about their day-long wait in the courtroom.

The arbitrary and capricious nature of our judicial system's attitude is also made unmistakably clear through sentencing. Since the law gives judges broad discretion, it is not unusual to find that on one and the same day the judge sitting in AR1 is letting prostitutes off with Time Served while just across the hall, in AR2, another judge is sentencing another group of women, who have committed an identical offense, to five days on Rikers Island. This is further complicated by the individualistic way in which the judge who sits in night court (6 P.M. to 2 A.M.) and the judge who sits on the bench during the "lobster shift" (2 A.M. to 10 A.M.) handle prostitution arrests.

For example, on February 17, 1983, one judge sitting in day court was sentencing prostitutes to Time Served while the other was giving sentences of five days on Rikers Island. That evening the night court judge was handing out fines of one hundred dollars or fifteen days in jail, while on the lobster shift, women were receiving sentences of hundred dollar fines or ten days in jail.

On any given day it is possible to visit arraignment court and observe this kind of diversity in the handling of prostitution cases. What is inescapable is the impression that each judge acts out his or her own attitude toward women accused of this misdemeanor. Were that not true, there would be far more diversity in the sentencing. In other words, each prostitution case coming before a particular judge would be handled individually and the penalty might vary from woman to woman, taking into account her previous arrest record, the details of the immediate arrest, or other factors that the judge thought important to consider before sentencing.

Over the years, we came to know some of the judges and began to understand the origin of the inconsistencies and inequities we observed in the sentencing process.

One judge was a relative newcomer to the bench. He was always kind and sometimes sympathetic to the women, never failing to treat them with respect, and was the only person sitting on the bench who addressed the women (and all other prisoners) by name. He would invariably say, "Miss _____, do you have anything to say before I impose sentence?" always looking directly at her.

One day over drinks we asked about his feelings toward the prostitution laws and their enforcement. In response he told us about his upbringing in an impoverished area of New York City, and his conviction that he could just as easily have become a criminal as a judge. He had remained in the neighborhood where he was born and had never forgotten the things he had seen on those streets. There was no doubt in his mind that most prostitution arrests are made illegally and he would be happy if prostitution were decriminalized. The way he dealt with those arrests was an honest reflection of his overall attitude: He sentenced women to Time Served.

A middle-aged judge we spoke to gave the appearance of being bored to death with his work; he seemed unaware that he was dealing with human beings. Despite that, he routinely sentenced prostitutes to Time Served. Then one day he changed and began giving straight jail time to every prostitution case. As a consequence, and in self-defense, women who came before him were pleading not guilty. However, he set no bail, just a trial date for them to return to court. He quickly developed a "hanging judge" reputation among prostitutes, who whenever possible would delay their arraignment to avoid his courtroom.

He readily agreed with us that prostitution should be decriminalized. The radical shift in his pattern of sentencing was a way of trying to force the issue. By imposing jail sentences, he expected that one of two things might happen. Either the women would plead not guilty in the hopes of getting a lesser sentence after a trial, thus clogging the court calendar and slowing down the whole judicial system. Or the women would continue to plead guilty, adding an additional burden to the already overcrowded facilities at Rikers Island. The result was to be a realization that our prostitution laws must be reexamined. However, this judge soon discovered that his caseload was just a drop in the bucket which failed to produce the result he sought, and soon thereafter he resumed sentencing prostitutes to Time Served.

A third judge had a reputation for imposing such harsh sentences that his name struck terror in the heart of every street prostitute in Manhattan. Having heard about him for years before ever seeing him in court, we discovered that the women had not exaggerated about the excessively punitive sentences they received from him. These were often coupled with a condescending attitude and a tendency toward ridicule.

Given his court behavior, we were shocked to discover that he, too, believed in the decriminalization of prostitution. He justified his punishment of prostitutes by stating that until the law changed, the "community" had a right to expect lawbreakers to be treated as such. He intended to continue harsh sentencing so it would be unmistakably clear that he was upholding the law, because the rights of the community outweighed his belief that prostitution was a victimless crime. He claimed to have been the recipient of letters and petitions complaining about the "coddling of criminals," an accusation that he took very much to heart in sentencing prostitutes.

Finally came the gentlest and most soft-spoken of judges. He interacted with all prisoners in his courtroom and routinely gave Time Served for prostitution violations. While admitting that he was uncertain about the decriminalization of prostitution, he was not prepared to punish women who violated that law.

While we hoped that the women on the bench might prove

more sympathetic, we discovered that they were as divided in their behavior as their male counterparts. One female judge insisted upon learning the time an arrest occurred, because she reserved her heaviest sentences for prostitutes who began work before midnight. Her intent was to protect ordinary citizens from exposure to their illicit activity. After stating her position, she sentenced women who were on the job at 10 P.M. to five days on Rikers Island, despite the fact that the location of their arrest was Eleventh Avenue, a construction site far removed from any residential area.

It is hard to forget the judge who glanced down at the prostitute at the bench, lifted her arrest record in the palm of his hand as though to weigh it, glanced and chuckled for the benefit of the public as his hand fell from its sheer weight, and then handed out a hefty sentence.

Other judges turned out to be preachers in disguise. One chastised and severely punished women who worked in the neighborhood where he lived, because their presence prevented his young daughter from walking down the street without encountering drug pushers and junkies. Another sentenced women to Time Served but warned that if they appeared before him again they would regret it; he suggested—without any regard for their training, skills, or the high unemployment rate —that they go find other jobs.

Certainly there were exceptions, but our overriding impression of judges was that they were indifferent to and refused to acknowledge the humanity and individuality of women who work as prostitutes. We came to understand that some ambitious judges—just like tricks, pimps, and cops—use the women as pawns and profit from their labors. A friendly judge explained how colleagues use prostitution cases as a means of moving up the judicial ladder. It seems that judges are evaluated, in part at least, on the basis of the number of cases they dispose of on a given day. In other words, if they arraign fifty people and forty plead guilty and are sentenced, only the remaining ten cases have been added to the already overburdened calendar of the trial courts. Thus, like cops, some judges have a vested interest in prostitutes' pleading guilty. This may help explain why we never heard judges raise questions about whether the women appearing before them had been legally arrested. Is it possible that they never wonder about the frequency with which prostitutes are repeatedly arrested? In the days before prearraignment was introduced, when arresting police officers appeared at arraignment, it was hard to avoid noticing the coziness of the relationships they had with the arrested women. Couple this with the number of times a particular cop appeared in court with a particular woman he had arrested on numerous prior occasions, and a problem—or at the very least a question—ought to have been raised in the minds of even the most disinterested of judges.

Let us be clear that we are not leveling a charge of judicial self-interest against *all* judges, but we are raising the possibility that it is a factor in the treatment of prostitutes by *some* judges.

Over time, women who used the church bus would often ask who was sitting on the bench that week. The information was valuable to them because they were occasionally able (by cajoling the police or court personnel) to delay their arraignment from one shift to another and avoid the most punitive judges. Or they might stay home a day rather than risk a harsh jail sentence. Eventually we devised a form which was posted on the bus each week. It listed the names of the judges sitting in day court, night court, and the lobster shift; the sentences they were giving for prostitution arrests; and how they were dealing with outstanding warrants in those instances where women had not paid fines for earlier convictions. So in addition to educating ourselves, and providing some minor comfort for women whom we encountered in court, we enabled other women to decide intelligently whether they wanted to risk arrest in light of the penalties being dispensed. In a small but not entirely insignificant way, this information empowered them.

As our visits to court increased, our knowledge of the system led us to encourage women whose arrests had not been legal to plead not guilty. However, the mythology of the punitive judge handing out unreasonable bail was too deeply rooted for us to overcome. Perhaps if the physical circumstances had been different and Legal Aid lawyers had more time to deal with the women individually, we might together have achieved a partial victory. But the circumstances of the environment worked against this. Although we did our best to encourage women to stand up for their rights, we were never able to persuade them that they had any.

Night after night we sat on the bus listening to women tell stories of illegal arrests, watching the streets, and observing the cops making those arrests. Yet at the same time it was painfully clear that there was no way in which we could organize the women to defend their rights under existing laws. In the absence of that kind of united protest, their ongoing victimization by the police and the courts would continue unabated, reinforcing a self-image of powerlessness. We concluded that the only intervention that would make a permanent difference was legal change. Only through such means would the police and the courts be deprived of the power they had to control the everyday lives of these women. We now recognized that accomplishment of such a goal required the aid and leadership of people and organizations that were perceived to be "respectable." Our next steps became clear.

7

Religion Demands Reform: "The Only Good Whore Is an Ex-Whore"

> I meet a lot of
> Saviors
> None with
> Any soul
> Their conscience
> Is in their socks
> Always . . .
> Left on
> Even in . . .
> Intimate moments
> At the railroad
> Always missing that
> Last train.
> —KIMBERLY

If there is another unique aspect to our work in the street, aside from its nonjudgmental and even sympathetic treatment of the working women, it is that the project was supported by Judson Church and based upon affirmations of the faith, which came out of the church's life. We neither hid nor trumpeted our religious connections, they were just there. And to the women they turned out to be more important than we realized.

In order to understand the church's contemporary stand on the issue of prostitution, we need a brief historical résumé. When people refer to prostitution as the world's oldest profession, it is not an idle description but a historical fact. In ancient times, prostitution had a certain stamp of approval. It obtained a legitimation in the service of religion. In the ancient religions of Phoenicia and Mesopotamia, and particularly in the cults of Canaan, there were what was known as "temple prostitutes" (male and female) in the service of the deities. Sexual rituals were performed in homage to the gods or goddesses, particularly the goddess of fertility, who made the crops grow and flourish, and increased the population.

There are numerous Biblical references to these cults and their religious prostitutes, who were encountered by the Israelites in their nomadic wanderings and captivities. Evidence exists that the Israelites, constantly influenced by these strange religions, adopted in early times some of the rituals of "cult prostitutes." However, in order to avoid assimilation and because the rites deteriorated into sexual orgies, Hebrew worship was reformed, and cult prostitutes were forbidden. The Deuteronomic laws contained strict rules against the practices of foreign and pagan religions.

It would seem that the Israelites' attitude toward noncultic prostitution was not as vehement and condemnatory. After all, in Old Testament history, prostitutes were somewhat superfluous since all women were little more than chattel owned by men. Concubines flourished and were socially acceptable; they performed physical and sexual labors for the patriarch of the family and his friends in exchange for bed and board, with some beads and baubles thrown in.

One of the ancient scriptural stories that illustrate a more tolerant understanding of prostitution tells of the harlot Rahab, a patriot who hid Israelite spies in her home. She became a heroine and her home was spared by God in the destructive war that engulfed her country. We find in the prophet Hosea's tirade against harlots the first blast against the sexual double standard. In his condemnation of the people of Israel for their unfaithfulness to God, Hosea says, "I will not punish your daughters for playing the wanton, nor your sons' brides for their adultery, because you *men* resort to wanton women and sacrifice with temple prostitutes." This prophet displayed an even-handed justice that isn't evident 2500 years later.

It was Jesus who in his ministry and teachings displayed an uncharacteristic tolerance and humanity toward "wanton women." He continuously shocked his followers and the religious folk of his time by suggesting that tax collectors and prostitutes would get into the Kingdom of God before them. His attitude did not influence the treatment of prostitutes in later societies, but he was probably responsible for what toleration and protection there was.

All through recorded history, societies and their laws have dealt with prostitutes. It was in the Roman Empire that prostitutes were first required to register. Their names were placed on an official registry and could never be removed. (A modern objection by prostitutes to legalization is precisely this ancient practice.) Roman prostitutes were also taxed, required to wear distinctive clothes, and deprived of many civil liberties that were guaranteed other Romans (the latter deprivation is in practice probably little different today in the U.S.). Roman law identified as prostitutes the inmates of brothels, those who offered their bodies for hire in taverns and elsewhere, those who made their living by furnishing sex for pay, and other promiscuous women generally, whether they took remuneration for their services or not. For the Romans, public display was an important ingredient in their notions about prostitution. (It might also be said that we twentieth-century moderns, whose morality is based more on aesthetics than on ethics, have not changed much on that score.)

Perhaps the most interesting of all treatments of prostitution in the history of the Western world was its proscription in canon law by the lawyers and lawgivers of the medieval church. In comparison to contemporary self-righteous diatribes against prostitutes by religious leaders, the canonistic proclamations were models of reasoned and balanced deliberation in contextual ethics. James A. Brundage, in a superb monograph on the subject, tells us that the canonists flatly disapproved of prostitution on scriptural and theological grounds, yet "their treatment of prostitution was strangely ambivalent. Although they disapproved in principle . . . still, in practice they were prepared to tolerate prostitution and justify its toleration in Christian society."* Of course, this toleration stems from the earlier teachings of St. Augustine on the subject. He believed that if it weren't for prostitutes and their services, the established patterns of sexual relationships would be endangered. So it was better to suffer prostitution with all its evils than try to eliminate it from society. This teaching is particularly interesting in the light of present-day local efforts to justify its criminalization on the basis of prostitution's destructiveness to the social fabric of family life.

Church law in the twelfth and thirteenth centuries dealt with the ethics of the prostitute's profession even though her status was considered debased. Though canonists based their decision primarily on Roman law, in some areas they went beyond the Romans. The medieval jurist, for example, tended to extend the definition and to identify certain occupations with prostitution —acting, for example.

The canonists' view of the female of the species is quite archaic by our standards, but it is important to understand their beliefs because it helps us to understand the legacy they passed on. They considered female sexuality different from male, declaring that woman was not created in the image of God, as was man. Several observations underlay their view of women's sexuality: (1) The chastity of women was always suspect because they were always ready for sexual intercourse. (2) Since women were so susceptible to sexual temptation, their sex life had to be properly structured and confined to married life. (3) Women were fickle and inconsistent creatures by nature and so were more easily led into sexual sins.

In spite of all this, women were expected to observe a more

*"Prostitution in Medieval Canon Laws" in *Signs: Journal of Women in Culture and Society* (University of Chicago Press), vol. 1, no. 4 (Summer 1976), p. 825.

stringent standard of sexual conduct than men. As much as we deplore the ignorance and prejudice of this view, it did produce more lenient attitudes and actions toward prostitutes. As far as these theological lawyers were concerned, prostitutes were culpable for their sin, but not too much so, because after all, they were simply acting naturally. Harsh punishments were reserved for pimps, procurers, and the keepers of brothels, who, making those services available, increased men's temptation!

The double standard—which grew, let us remember, out of the theology of the church—was perceived in many ways. For example, if a woman was impoverished and hungry, she was never justified in turning to prostitution, even to feed her children. However, in canon law, poverty could be an excuse for a man to steal, and under certain circumstances even homicide was vindicated. Prostitutes were so debased that they had no right to accuse anyone of a crime or even to own property. In spite of a certain leniency by the church in judging her sin, the worst disability that the medieval prostitute faced was the denial of any kind of social status or fundamental civil liberties. One doesn't have to be too observant to note that things haven't changed that much for today's prostitute in New York City. Could a prostitute in our society win a legitimate complaint of rape, or theft, or assault?

But the medieval church, though contemptuous of the prostitute's sinful ways, dealt ambivalently with some matters pertaining to her livelihood. For example, money given to a prostitute could not be reclaimed by the donor. What she *did* was wrong, but taking the money was no crime. Yet there was a disclaimer even in that right to keep the money earned—she must charge a "fair price" for her services. Further, the prostitute must not deceive a client in what she shows (a kind of medieval truth-in-packaging law).

But there was a more vexing and self-serving question for the church to deal with: the claim upon the prostitute's tithe. Could the wages of sin be acceptable as alms to the church? Some canon lawyers said no; some said that if it was held in escrow until she reformed, then it was acceptable. Still other legal ethicists reasoned that if money was got by force or threat of force, it was not acceptable, but other "ill-gotten gains, derived from more or less generous, if misdirected, impulses," were legitimate offerings. The earnings of prostitutes and actresses fell into this category. The casuistry of the church was always at its best when it was justifying a practice that was morally and theologically abhorrent but pragmatically necessary, whether it was laundering "dirty money," excusing human slavery, or justifying war.

One more attitude had its religious origins in this time. Though the prostitute was a weak and powerless person, socially degraded, ecclesiastically cast out, it was still possible for her to reform and attain salvation (as did Mary Magdalen). There were two ways the medieval church held out for "harlots" to reform: to become a nun and join a religious order, or to marry. Special religious orders worked to redeem prostitutes, but it was considered by the church to be the most difficult of all conversions. One thing was clear—leaving the life, repenting of her ways, and living a godly life were the only way a prostitute could be accepted by the church or have her rights and liberties restored. The medieval church laid the groundwork for the modern (Protestant and Catholic) church's theological and moral views toward prostitution.

Any attempt to understand the contemporary church's view of prostitute and prostitution without reviewing its attitude toward sexuality itself would be somewhat fruitless.

The church after the Reformation did not much alter its highly restrictive view of the nature of sexual activity. One of the reasons for the castigation of prostitutes was that sex had only one purpose: procreation; and only one context: marriage. All other reasons for sex were sinful. In time, Protestantism moved beyond the view that the only valid purpose of sex was reproduction, but it did not move beyond the understanding that the only proper context was marriage. It was difficult for even Luther and Calvin to believe that a good Creator would have endowed us with the marvelous capacity for sex with one another only for the means of procreation of the species. Though our Protestant forebears might have been loath to grant us too much pleasurable satisfaction from the doing of it, nevertheless within the strict confines of monogamous marriage it was an allowable joy.

Later in contemporary Christianity, as contextual ethics dealt with the changing mores and practices of the modern world, sexual activity was found by some to be permissible outside marriage provided there was a responsible love and commitment by both partners. But in most Christian churches, we haven't dealt with sexuality at all, hoping that its problems would go away, praying that our children will be immune to it until they are ready for marriage or a "responsible commitment," and deploring all signs of what is seen as sexual deviancy.

One could maintain that the church's ambiguity about sexual matters, if not downright avoidance, exemplifies the same puzzling paradox as sex in human life. Sex sometimes is a hallowing and renewing experience, but just as often it is distracting, coercive, frivolous, and even boring. It is at one and the same time deadly serious and terribly funny. Our sexuality has the power to increase our knowledge about ourselves and the world, but at the same time it is capable of producing in us fears and phobias that paralyze and even terrorize us. It is little wonder that the church, which habitually thinks in absolute or categorical terms, might have had a difficult time handling this complicated aspect of our human existence, and preferred to remain silent. But its silence was not total, and those who preferred to be vocal based their ethical and moral approbations on post-theological dogma, the proof-texting of ancient Scripture to support what ostensibly was and is an antisex bias or at best a highly confined and restrictive view of sexual pleasure.

It might be instructive to look at two aspects of sexuality that are prevalent in our time, and with which the church has had great difficulty. The first is homosexuality.

Now, there is a word that tends to strike fear and outrage into the hearts of even the most kindly and liberal persons. And the church, with the help of the Jerry Falwells and Phyllis Schlaflys, finds itself involved in the most schismatic and controversial issue since the debate on slavery. There is no way for us, inside or outside the church, to avoid the matter, and what is remarkable is how long we were able to postpone even the recognition of a group of people, a way of life, that is as old as human history, and more popular than any one of us wants to know. When you consider that one out of every twenty adults is homosexual (and about one in every six men), it seems almost impossible that only recently did we begin to talk about them. However, the reason for the ignorance and the neglect may be evident. Intolerance of homosexuality translates into repression; repression encourages invisibility; invisibility and stereotypes go together.

A place to begin in our understanding of the issue is with the realization that the so-called homosexual problem is more than likely a heterosexual problem. We have learned in these past years that what was labeled the "Negro problem" is basically the problem of white racism. As the "woman problem" is primarily that of male sexism. It should be remembered that all the old familiar scriptural references that were used to exclude and denigrate the blacks in another generation are the same kind of Biblical justifications used to castigate and excommunicate gays and lesbians from full participation in society and in the life of the church today.

Homosexuality is a radical threat to all those who believe that the "orders of creation" are fixed and absolute and the sexual structures of our human existence a given. Homosexuality brings home the lesson that there are varieties in our sexual life (just as in all other created existence)—that is, different ways of showing love and affection for people of the same sex. The church ought to know, better than most, that this incredible variety in the human family—colors, cultures, languages, mores —must be nurtured not in some easy tolerance but from a sacred conviction that all of us in our marvelous multiformity are children of God, whose rights are inviolable and whose respect is guaranteed.

For centuries, our Jewish and Christian institutions condemned, punished, and castrated homosexuals, even put them to death, giving our present legal tradition its religious and moral legacy. That tradition is the church's shame—not just the severity of the reaction to the particular group but the denial of love and acceptance that these religious traditions mandate for all human beings. The real religious challenge facing those who claim these traditions is not reconciling the acceptance of homosexuals with certain Scripture passages but rather how to reconcile the continuing condemnation, ostracism, and even cruelty toward homosexuals with our message of love and justice. The burden of proof today is on those who would perpetuate a theology and a policy of demeaning condescension and second-class citizenship in the congregations of our synagogues and churches; and on those who say that persons of faith who are gay are not just different from those who are straight but that gays are certified by the church to be sinfully different.

If the truth were known, the category "sinfully different" has as much to do with the sexual life-styles of many homosexuals —variegated, casual, and multiple sex activities—as it has to do with the partners' being of the same sex. This accounts for the fundamentalist preachers jumping on AIDS as God's incarnate retribution and ultimate rejection of homosexuals and their way of life. It was a sign of God's progressive nature that rather than destroy whole cities such as Sodom and Gomorrah (substitute New York and San Francisco), he created a selective form of punishment: only for those who were the source of his anger (well, almost only those!). More on sexual styles and the church's intolerance later. Suffice it to say that from our place in the religious community we are not persuaded by all the scriptures, all the sermons and treatises, that homosexuality is any ground for exclusion from the church, or from candidacy for ordination, or from missionary activity of the larger church. Such exclusionary attitudes are inconsistent with the belief that God's creation is as large and diverse as life itself, and we prefer to meet all God's people on the ground of our common humanity rather than on the rungs of a divine hierarchical ladder where some sexual preferences are closer to God's will than others.

The larger society may be evolving to a more tolerant behavior toward this deviancy in human sexuality, and certainly important legal advances have occurred, but the church is still far from acceptance of homosexuality as an alternate life-style.

Equally difficult for the church to deal with, in past and present, is serendipitous sex. Moral theory, categories, and axioms are easy to handle because they are mental images with which we are at home. We have a moral way of seeing that automatically envisions certain behavior as wrong or sinful. If we are ethical atheists, we might say the behavior is contextually in error. One of the real dangers of moving into territory such as the illicit working world of prostitutes with a certain nonjudgmental openness is that one may oneself be subject to change. We moved into that strange and forbidden world with many of the prejudices that the "square world" shared with us. One can harbor those biases without being accusatory toward those who violate our precepts. In this instance it was our sexual precepts that were at stake. As long as we can keep people and their behavior within the confines of certain imagined constructs and they fit *our* view of reality, we feel safe and secure. For example, if we see the prostitute's view of sex as perverse, repugnant, and sick, the result of mental illness, emotional distress, or economic victimization, then we can accept and even pity her. When people, problems, ways of life break out of their constructs, our world is shaken up. In the prostitutes' working lives and in their views of sex, they challenged and questioned all our well-established views of human sexuality.

In the world of recreational sex, where intimate pleasures are bartered, one encounters different concepts of sexuality. For example, one finds among prostitutes attitudes that could be characterized as the "desacralization" of sex. In the Jewish and Christian understanding of sexual ethics, sex is a holy, set-apart activity appropriate only in the most restrictive context. This moral view treats sex as the mysterious and powerful aspect of our lives that it is; its potency upon our body, mind, and emotions dictates its use with care. Some would say that sex is only appropriate where the mind has framed its ethical reasonableness and the heart has vowed its loving commitments. Most of us either were raised on this moral perception of sex with its religious judgments or else we received this view of sex by osmosis from class and cultural mores.

"On the stroll," the women, who bargain for sexual pleasures, make sex the mundane and earthy aspect of our lives that it also is. Sex in their world is not some mysterious and sacred rite, a consummation of romantic love; sex between consenting adults may be as casual as a friendly handshake.

When a prostitute talks about sex, it is funny, ludicrous, sad, weird, fumbling, and flaky. She deromanticizes sex, disarms it, so that it is not some momentous, secret act with which we are going to consummate our humanity. Her attitude toward sex is much more mundane and fortuitous—sometimes healing, usually hedonistic. She has seen too much: macho jocks turned into quivering little boys who can't get it up, impotent husbands finally getting it off in a therapeutic experience of oral-genital sex. (She may not be licensed as a sex therapist, but she has a lot of the qualifications and many a satisfied client.)

The frightening aspect of this offhand view of sex is that it raises a most troublesome question: If sex is not mysterious and unique, how can we keep it under control? The keepers of our socioreligious codes, at least in sermons and ethical texts, would have us believe that sex, separated from responsible love and long-term commitment, is "dehumanizing" and "animal-like." The fact that most of us believe that, without ever assessing contrary evidence, is a testimony to the way in which we accept most popular dogmas and myths in our culture, whether they are theological or sociological.

Sex in prostitution is a matter-of-fact, daily occurrence where biological desire and economic needs meet. This cursory and somewhat organic way of seeing sex is part of the prostitute's life-style and one of the reasons she is able to do her business without being drowned in emotional ambivalence. There is some evidence that more and more people who are not prostitutes are treating sex in this manner, but they are subject to none of the social ostracism and moral condemnation of the prostitute.

The religious attitude toward sex hasn't changed, simply the practice. In more modern and liberal religious terminology, sex is a form of "covenanting" and "communion," of "intimate bonding." Sex outside of responsibility and discipline is judged by the church and most psychologists to be alienating, debilitating, and sometimes destructive. Whether the activity of a "brief encounter" is homosexual or heterosexual doesn't matter. It is casual sex that is judged. The prostitute in her work is very clear that she means nothing by her offer or her act other than the temporary granting of sexual gratification, much as a masseuse gives bodily pleasure in the massaging of the body.

Another reason for the castigation of the prostitute's work by moralists is that she is "selling her body," and since the body is inseparable from the rest of her, this is denigration of the body's worth. The prostitute does not think of her work in this way, but feels that she is performing a service or bartering a technique. The fact that the service she performs or the pleasure she provides entails the use of her body cannot be the real reason for religion's or society's disgust and revulsion at her work. There is too much approved and high-price entertainment in which people use their bodies, sometimes abusively and brutally, often

in a detached and disconnected manner, to bring others enjoyment and pleasure. Boxing, football, hockey, and wrestling
come immediately to mind. There has to be a deeper and more
complex reason for the repugnancy of the prostitute's work and
the universality of her rejection. Is she anathema to us because
she seems to threaten our cherished views about sex?

It is hard for us to deal with the possibility that sex is enjoyable
without genuine love or a long-term commitment. But if people
are honest about their experiences, anyone who ever fantasized
in a satisfactory masturbatory act or found sex fulfilling in a brief
encounter with a person he or she never saw again has some
evidence that such enjoyment is possible.

If sex without all the confinements we have prescribed for its
appropriateness—if such sex is possible and enjoyable, even if
not ultimately desirable, then many a foundation is shaken by
the very concept of serendipitous sex. The prostitute, then, is
not just a sexual pariah playing on our forbidden desires, but a
living, walking threat to every traditional moral and religious
belief that asserts romantic love, or monogamous marriage or
relationships, to be the exclusive fitting forms for any sexual
activity.

Could it be that the real reason religionists and moralists and
all the keepers of the codes scapegoat the prostitute so inhu-
manely is that in her manner of dealing with sex she has revealed a side of ourselves we have refused to admit? The prostitute's presence is troublesome precisely because she suggests
that the sexual act unaccompanied by all the moral strictures of
religious traditions may feel good and not be wrong; may be
enjoyable and not be destructive. She points to something we
cannot allow ourselves (or more particularly our offspring) to
think about—that casual sex can be good in the simple context
of an equivalent need, honestly communicated and mutually
responded to by two people. Could it be that the prostitute
forces us to entertain the thought that there is more than one
kind of sex and that neither is "right" or "wrong"? It would be

easier to understand our continuous attempts to ostracize, if not
be rid of, this incarnate danger to the moral and religious status
quo if this were the real reason for our unforgiving repudiation
of prostitution—that its practitioners are a genuine threat to the
church's major teaching about sex, which has shaped the mores
and legal restraints that dominate American attitudes toward
human sexual activity.

It is very important for us to understand the differences between the prostitute's valuation of sex and what may be the
majority perspective on the place of sexual activity in our lives.
The judgment from church and society that falls so heavily on
her head can only be a result of her mores' challenging some
of the fundamentals of this most potent and perplexing aspect
of our lives, our sexual nature. At least the excessive reaction to
the prostitute's life-style is more tolerable if it is seen as the
product of fear rather than anger. And nothing is more fearful
to the priest than that his faith not be true, or to the moralist
than that her ethics are not supported by logic and reason.

This has been made more than clear to us in these latter years
by the Moral Majority and their religious allies. They are frightened that America's drift toward permissiveness and promiscuity in recent years will destroy us, and they have sought to
tighten the laws that threaten our valued traditions. These "traditions," for what may be obvious reasons, are centered around
the sexual activities of women—birth control, abortion, sex outside marriage, and recreational sex. The solution of these protectors of our values is to make laws that curtail if not forbid the
changing sexual mores in our society. Religion has always been
a major force in the control of sex. Anything that threatens that
control is interpreted as dangerous to society.

It would not be fair to expose the larger church's judgmental
and reformist position regarding prostitution without trying to
say something about the theological and ethical views that informed our own work with prostitutes. Judson Memorial
Church has been typed as a "liberal church" practically since

its beginning. There were different reasons in different periods for being labeled in this way. In the early twentieth century, when mainline Protestantism saw its mission to the immigrant population as basically the evangelization of foreigners, helping them to become good melting-pot Americans—that is, good Protestant Christians—Judson, which began as a mission church in Greenwich Village, refused to proselytize the local Italian-American immigrants, many of whom were Catholic. It served these Italian immigrants in every conceivable kind of economic, educational, and cultural ministry, but refused to be a WASP hotbed of evangelism. For evangelicals and particularly for our Baptist denomination at the turn of the century, the church was seen as liberal. In the 1920s and '30s, when the conventional church's main task was preaching and teaching the Gospel, and praying for the urban hordes of non-Christians in the great metropolis of New York, Judson was engaged in the support of early labor unions, and soup kitchens for the poor. It slept Depression victims on pews in the sanctuary, and encouraged intellectual and political dialogue from its open pulpit. During the 1950s and '60s, when the church in America was busy recovering liturgy and studying theology, Judson was involved in work with disturbed teenagers and heroin addicts; marching and protesting in civil rights demonstrations; becoming a home for the avant-garde arts; and helping women attain safe and secure abortions when it was illegal.

The church in history has always lost its power to judge and discern—when it consorted with the power of the state in society, and wanted to keep company with the right people. The church failed when it embraced only the cultured norms, in flagrant denial of what it knew to be its transcendent values, and when it sold its birthright for a mess of societal acceptance. For Judson Church, our work with prostitutes is in line with a stream of ministries that have preceded us for the past thirty years. In the 1950s, the scapegoats of our community and others throughout urban America were "juvenile delinquents," who were blamed for most everything wrong that happened. We gave them sanctuary, furnished them with social clubs, defended them when the police hassled them. They were not the children of our congregation—they were tough, sometimes violent, often troubled, Italian-American teenagers. Then we worked with heroin addicts, fought for their humanization, picketed City Hall for hospital beds so they could be treated as people in need rather than criminals. In the '60s we stood with blacks, protesters, and people who hated the war. In many instances they were not "our people," but we learned from their lives and their struggles. In the late '60s, it was women being criminalized for getting abortions. We identified with them, supported them, and conspired with them to break the law that we believed was unconstitutional, in order that they might exercise the God-given right of freedom of choice.

It would be hard for us to speak of a particular theology that led us or motivated us to work with prostitutes. But we should mention and pay tribute to some ecclesiological foundations that were laid in the late '40s, at the time when Judson began to find new life. There were two young ministers who started to build a new congregation of people. And there were two fundamental ingredients in the foundations on which a new church would grow: (1) The church existed primarily for those who were not in it. The world, and not the congregation, was the basis of ministry. (2) There was no issue or people in society so controversial or so difficult that the church should not be there—responding to every human crisis and need, wherever people were being mistreated or were suffering injustice. Judson's readiness to enter those controversial fields of endeavor that have marked its ministries over the past years has been in no small measure due to those two significant affirmations of the congregation.

In order to speak of our work today with prostitutes, we should make clear that the larger Christian Church in the history of its ministry has manifested a *pastoral* and *prophetic* function in its work in the world. The pastoral function might best be understood as *being there* for people in a nonproselytizing, nonjudgmental way. This has been referred to in theological circles as a "ministry of presence." It is a ministry difficult for the church, for it is a ministry without preaching or exhorting or trying to convert. For us, it is just being there on the streets where the women work, in the courts where they are judged and sentenced. It is a "ministry of immersion": We are immersed in their lives, feeling their pain, sensing their indignation, accepting their resentments—being there as an accepting, loving presence. Howard, as a minister (though their acceptance of him was a long time coming), is important to them. He has baptized their babies, married them, and perhaps most important, he has officiated at their memorial services when they were killed. In those moments of great tragedy and senseless violence, it was more important than at any other time that the church's presence be felt—for the church to say that in death as in life we are here for you, and your death is to be marked and your life remembered.

It was a memorial service that drew the prostitutes and the church closer together. On September 15, 1980, a woman named Bonnie was beaten, tortured, then murdered in the Queens apartment she shared with her man, James Parker. He had also been murdered, but his body was found elsewhere. At the women's request, we held a memorial service at Judson Church at seven o'clock in the morning. It may have been an unlikely hour for us squares, but it was the right time for the working women, who had just finished the Saturday night shift. It was the first time that most of them had been near a church for quite a while. Most of them had been written off, read out, excommunicated by their respective churches a long time before. But they gathered for this occasion, a little bleary-eyed, some still in their working garb. They came to pay their respects to a friend on the stroll. Howard spoke at her service.

Life seems no more precarious than when we receive news that a friend is dead. This past week our senses have been assaulted, our orderly mental processes have been torn by the irrational act that took our friend Bonnie from us.

We want this morning to remember Bonnie—to mourn her violent and unnecessary death, but also to remember and give thanks for her life. Some of you only knew her slightly or for a short time. Some knew her only at work, and others of you were close companions. Each of you has your own testimony of what she meant to you. Through this kaleidoscope of personal experiences, the reality of Bonnie is seen. Here this morning, the sadness of her death is mixed with gladness for her life.

I want to say a few words about Bonnie, whose Christian name was Karen Sheets. Bonnie was her street name. She was one of the first women we met when we started stopping on Lexington Avenue with the church mobile unit.

She was, on the surface, a tough and street-wise veteran, but just beneath the surface there was an incredible shyness that bespoke a fear of her own vulnerability to the dangers of the street. I saw in her a fierce loyalty to those she cared about. Since I did not know her well but for only too short a time, I will leave more personal remembrances to her close friends.

But I do want to say why I think this moment is significant. First, because though her funeral was held down South in her home, her parents and relatives did not share her life, for she long since had broken with her culture and home ties. Some of you here were her family, and I'm grateful that we can have this service with integrity, knowing her and what she did and giving thanks for her life. For we know that the way she worked as a prostitute did not for a moment diminish her worth as a human being. We have a God who is no respecter of persons—that is, God doesn't rate us according to our occupation, or what other people think of us, or how important we are. We are all God's children, and brothers and sisters to each other. And Bonnie's life was individually and uninterchangeably precious in His sight.

Last Sunday, during our church retreat, I announced Bonnie's tragic death to our congregation. In speaking of it, I said I sometimes feel like I have two congregations, one here at the church and one on the bus. But, I said, maybe it won't always be like that. And in some strange and mysterious way, in Bonnie's death strangers meet and comfort one another and pray together and remember a common friend—and we will never be completely separate congregations again.

Our pastoral ministry, apart from being there, means helping when we are asked. Giving information when it is needed. Advising on health problems; taking the women to the hospital when they are beaten up; protecting and sheltering them from a violent pimp or an outraged trick; visiting them in prison or hospital. These elements of the pastoral ministry are familiar to the church in its work with "normal" parishioners, but they do not often extend to outsiders. Perhaps it ought to be confessed here that this ministry was not a one-way street; they ministered to us. Be assured that we do not teach them nearly as much about ethics as we might think. Consider the woman who makes a promise not to hold out money on her man, then he abuses her and she is tempted to break her vow, but she refuses because she says simply, "I made a promise." (We break up marriages for less.) Or consider the tenacious loyalty of the prostitute as she comes to the aid of another streetwalker in danger, even though she is courting physical violence to herself. Or, in the face of society's contempt and even hatred of her presence, you find a woman taking it in her stride, filled with self-respect and a certain joy in life (not all the women, but enough to make you notice). They gave us something that meant a lot to us "square outsiders" who represented, albeit unwillingly, the society and the church that condemned. The women accepted us, and on occasions demonstrated their love and respect.

The reason society and the larger church can treat prostitutes as they do is because they have dehumanized, depersonalized, and stereotyped them into an inhuman category. The majority has always been adept at such stereotyping. It is a way of making a group inconsequential, even invisible. The prostitute makes that a little harder for us because she is brash in her public display, on occasions uninhibited in her dress, and insistent on her right to be on a public street doing what she does. We may depersonalize her, but she makes it difficult for us to ignore her. The stereotyping was overcome for us when by being there on the streets we got to know Michele, Martha, Sherre, Diane, and Kitty. Only when stereotypes have names and troubles, worries, fears, and sometimes joys, do we grant them humanity. The pastoral aspect of our ministry enabled us to get close, to know them as people like ourselves; their problems and difficulties may be different from yours and mine, but their humanity always manages to shine through.

Another aspect of the church's ministry is what has been called the *prophetic* one. The church has not always been at home with this function of ministry. The pastoral function is personal, dealing with an individual's needs and crises without any larger reference. The church has always been better at giving poor people food baskets at Christmas than at asking the larger question of the causes of their poverty. Judson Church's concept of ministry has been that the pastoral caring for and serving of people in need is insufficient without prophetic judgment of the social conditions that created their need. A strong motivation for our reaching out to these particular working women was the manner in which society treated them.

A prophetic ministry is one that affirms the pastoral but includes the larger issue—the systemic one. One can't deal with a prostitute's pain and frustration very long without realizing that her situation is an effect caused by social relations, laws, expectations, and other norms that make her what she is. As an individual, she does the work of a prostitute for any number of complicated reasons, but she is criminalized for only one reason —society's law labels her a criminal. Now, the church plays its part in this systemic judgment because its theology and morality have helped shape such laws. So perhaps the church's first act in its prophetic ministry should be to ask why society demands this retribution for prostitutes. We ought to probe, for example, the reasons for the perennial cleanup campaigns, beyond the political public relations. In New York City, for example, is City Hall truly morally offended by peep shows, streetwalkers, and massage parlors? Do our moral guardians really care about the people who live in that district?

In 1976, was the real reason for the antiprostitution solicitation law really to make our streets safe and inoffensive for the delegates to the Democratic convention? The politicians and community leaders, and the theater world of Times Square, joined in warning us that prostitutes were destroying their neighborhood, and creating a public threat to an otherwise tranquil and upstanding city.

When we listen to these kinds of reformers, we are reminded of certain ironies in our society's attitudes toward displays of sex. When the 1976 law against street solicitation was passed and many people in the theater business were sounding off against the women, *The Best Little Whorehouse in Texas* was playing on Broadway. It seems that prostitutes are O.K. if they are on stage or confined to our fantasies, but when they appear as real people on the street, they offend our sensibilities and are bad for show business.

However, whatever the facts are, whether this "oldest profession" is a public threat or a cause for declining theater receipts and fear in the streets, the good politician always knows what the people are clamoring for. There never was a Caesar worth his salt who didn't know when to give the people "circuses." The trouble with circuses, instead of solutions, is that they are dangerous digressions that prevent us from dealing with reality.

The legislators in Albany heard the people's cry, and their "circus" was the antisolicitation law, a "streetcleaning" bill that turned the police into moral sanitation workers. But that bill, even if it were not a violation of constitutional rights, is wrong because it is an unenforceable and irrelevant statute. More than that, it is wrong because it was and is a political charade that pretends to deal with a social problem about which most politicians know little and care less.

The church in its prophetic stance ought always to be suspicious and on guard when society attempts to deal with its "undesirables," and particularly when it makes laws to get rid of them. Who are these people? Who labels them? And who decides that they are the problem? The church in its original state was made up of undesirables of one kind or another. It ought, out of its own sense of history, and its compassion, to be ready to question a system that labels and denigrates a particular group of people, especially women who are voiceless and without political protection.

In this case, once again, politicians and the public play out an ancient charade—finding someone or something to blame and passing a law against it: a law fallacious in its assumptions, dishonest in its pretense to a solution, and dangerous in its scapegoating mentality. The McCall-Ohrenstein bill was no more successful at ridding us of prostitution than was the Rockefeller get-tough drug statute in ridding our streets of drug dealers and addicts. The mythology around prostitutes and the Times Square area makes it easy to lay the burden of a hundred years on the highly visible streetwalker and the entourage of accompanying exhibitionists. But put some of them in a Broadway theater or a chic East Side club, add a little music, and people will pay a premium to see them.

Almost a decade after the bill, the cleanup campaign still goes on, but nothing has changed except the locales where the women work. The prostitutes are forced into more dangerous and isolated areas, but the addicts and street hustlers are still all around us.

The ensuing years seem to have revealed the more truthful reason for cleaning up Times Square, and it is far more extensive than making theatergoers feel safer. It is a whole new "urban removal" scheme. Its campaign slogan might be "Ban the blight! Move it uptown or move it downtown—but *move* it." Several years ago, when the Forty-second Street Redevelopment Corporation came into existence, the true roots of the city's moral indignation were exposed. The real aim for the cleanup is to make the Times Square area more profitable for a different group of people! That would mean tearing down the old familiar facade with its shabby and repulsive exterior and erecting a new setting capable of housing million-dollar hotels and restaurants and fashionable luxury condominiums. Saving the morals of this town is sloganeering sham when the real intent is to replace porno flicks and massage parlors, prostitutes and drug dealers, with another kind of money-making power. People who speak disparagingly about a "million-dollar porn business" aren't really concerned about the financial rip-off. Rather, it is that the people doing it have a seedy and unsavory product. In other words, the wrong people have control of the territory. They'll have to go, and if some people lose their rights or their livelihood in the process, so be it. The powers that be, who know what is best for us, have to *restore* this area, which has the potential for funneling billions of dollars into the "right pockets." Pious talk about "quality-of-life crime" ought not to turn the head of the church, making it believe that moving prostitutes around this city, as well as in and out of jail, like pawns on a chess table, has nearly as much to do with morality as it does with money and property.

There is an interesting sidelight on the present battle over Times Square and its reclamation for the right people. In an earlier period in this city, prostitution was confined to certain neighborhoods—usually poor ones and minority enclaves. In the first part of the twentieth century, Harlem was the "black tenderloin." Black prostitutes stayed in Harlem. Prostitution was no alien thing to black women, who have been sexually exploited since slavery. In every Southern city in the 1920s and

'30s, the red-light district was on the other side of the tracks in the black ghetto, and young white boys "discovered their manhood" with the help of the "two-dollar whore." Prostitutes and houses of ill repute were integrating blacks and whites long before there was a civil rights movement. In New York City, it was not until the early 1960s, when Harlem became inhospitable to visiting whites, that black prostitutes moved downtown to pursue their trade. Most civic leaders and today's reformers date the deterioration of Times Square to when the black prostitutes and ghetto street youth discovered the Forty-second Street stop on the A train. How much of today's ardent crusade to clean up Times Square has to do with sexual morality, and how much is sometimes disguised racism, is hard to delineate.

Also, any prophetic stance worthy of its legacy would have to question the almost unanimous public and media scapegoating of "the pimp" as the *sole* parasite living off the prostitute's work. Aren't there any other opportunists taking her money and using her profession? As a matter of fact, there are a number of people living off the woman's body and reaping gains from her profession. There is the owner of the "hot-sheet hotel" where the prostitute takes her trick. He charges her ten dollars for an average use of fifteen minutes in a sleazy, unkempt, and run-down hostelry. It doesn't take a computer to calculate the profit for a small hotel with only ten rooms at those rates. Or there is the policeman. He lives off her work, not by taking payoffs, but in the overtime he receives from chasing women and spending time in the clogged courtrooms awaiting disposition of their cases. In the late 1970s, policemen working the vice squad were making as much as five hundred dollars a week in overtime. Then there is the judiciary, representing the state, taking its share. When the judge in the courtroom fines the woman five hundred dollars and gives her ten days to pay, he becomes what Inspector Richard Dillon, formerly of the New York City vice squad, calls "the biggest pimp of all." Add to this the fact that on the stroll, in many bars and coffee shops, she pays more than the average person, and has none of the usual courtesies and rights.

Man, it was the coldest night of the year. I was freezin' out here and that motha-fuckin' Shorty he closed his coffeehouse and wouldn't let us ho's in. He be takin' our money all the time, glad to have us in there. But now he don't want us. That ain't right. With that shit he serves, he be lucky to have anybody there. That place be downright dirty. But it's warm on a cold night. And he ain't got no right to shut us out.

In the female prostitute we see the marginal and the powerless being victimized by a system that has censured her life-style and criminalized her work. And the church, in its best prophetic tradition, must question the system that uses its vast power to single out a particular class of working women to label and chastise.

In the Christian tradition, Jesus is the master teacher for the followers of the Way. He warned us not to be taken in by any pretext to goodness or devoutness, for many times this covers the worst of all sins—pride and hypocrisy. He found his company in the rough-and-tumble of ordinary folks scratching for a living out of the sea and the earth—people whose sins and shortcomings would most likely be of the flesh. From them, in their unworthiness and unpretentiousness, Jesus confirmed that the truly venal sins are not of the flesh but of the spirit—pride, arrogance, superiority. This is not to claim that Jesus would approve of prostitution as an exemplary vocation, any more than he did fishing and tax collecting, from which work he called some of his disciples.

Agnes sat in the bus late on a hot Friday night in August, cooling her heels, and avoiding arrest. She talked of spiritual things. Her theological questions were laced with scatological exhortations. Her eyes pleaded with the minister for some confirmation that her nightly exercise of praying, even though she was a prostitute, was heard by God.

Now, I ain't no hypocrite 'cause I never promised to give it up, but will I burn in hell for what I do? That's what they say! I don't rob and steal and I tries to give a man his money's worth. What do you think, preacher, am I headed for hell?

The church's temptation throughout her history has always been to convert and reform, but Jesus told us in a hundred ways that what is required of us is to be there for others, and particularly those whom society has cast out as unworthy of any human dignity and value. If the church can countenance among its members bigots, liars, hypocrites, adulterers, usurers, and many who make their living off other people's miseries, then it should be able to embrace and accept the prostitute, who simply lives off the needs and desires of others. She does not pretend that her work is noble or character-building. She knows it is just a hard job, with long hours and a lot of grief.

Prostitutes are a class of human beings whom the church and society have treated as people who need to be punished for what they are, just as, in other times, the church punished fornicators, homosexuals, scientists, and theological heretics. Most of these "sins" for which the church condemned and the state punished are now forgivable, if not acceptable. And many such people are in the church and active in its life. Perhaps it is time that the church accepted those who work in recreational sex as part of the diversity of life-styles and occupations that make up its congregations. The working prostitute will then become part of the community of faith, just as her patron has always been.

Epilogue:
Where Do We Go from Here?
Signposts Toward a Wise and More
Humane Public Policy

I look ahead, I look
back
and I see the same
love
destruction
power
corruption
energy
faith
hate
Then again there is
birth
I look ahead to the
time when there
is nothing to look
back on
—SUSAN

In 1971, several years before *Roe* v. *Wade,* the Supreme Court's landmark decision on abortion, the State of New York in a courageous act of pioneering legislation declared that women in New York would no longer be labeled criminal for exercising their personal right to terminate their own pregnancies. One wonders what the future holds for another social issue, which, while not an identical problem, bears some striking parallels.

We have a law regarding prostitutes that, if not in its essence, at least in its application and enforcement, criminalizes *women* for the choice of an act that is primarily personal and intimate. Even when the bartering for sex is public, as in streetwalking, the solicitation is harmless and much less offensive and obnoxious than what men say publicly to many women every day on the streets of the city. It is a law against women of which men are the creators, enforcers, and violators.

This law tells women that there are certain kinds of work they may not do, whether it hurts anyone else or not. Though one is hard-pressed to draw any lines between types of jobs in the sex industry, *streetwalkers* are arbitrarily singled out for penalties and punishment. So the heavy hand of the law falls almost exclusively on the poorest in the trade, and the pattern is not only sex discrimination (male prostitutes and transsexual prostitutes are relatively untouched) but also racial discrimination: black women are arrested and arraigned out of proportion to their relative numbers on the street.

As was pointed out earlier, we have a law that by merely labeling a woman forces her into a criminal subculture and strips her of the rights she is entitled to as a citizen of this nation. She may be raped, beaten, and molested by other people—even the police—and have little recourse because of her "label." She may be murdered, and many times her violent demise raises little notice. She is frequently the victim of preventive detention, a form of crime control we have resisted in this democracy because it is an affront to every conception of civil liberty. A known thief, or a known rapist, or a chronic robber/mugger cannot be picked up by police and detained without evidence that convinces a jury or a judge that the person is guilty of a criminal act. But the women of the streets are frequently arrested without any proof that they are breaking the law.

Any law that in its application dehumanizes and brutalizes one whose only crime is indulging for pay the sexual fantasies of our brothers, fathers, and sons is not worthy of a civilized society. No matter how morally repugnant or religiously sinful prostitution may appear to the majority, no nation can long treat a segment of its citizenry like this without forsaking its most valuable asset—its avowed belief in and protection of human rights.

The prostitute is, indeed, an indentured servant, a slave, but not to her sexual occupation. She is held hostage by the *law,* which strips her of her personal rights, so that she may be arrested anywhere, anytime, not because of what she has done, but because of who she is. We are told that a civilization may be judged by how it treats the weakest and most defenseless among its people. It would be hard for us to find a group in our society whose rights are more violated, whose dignity is more denigrated, and whose work is made more miserable than "streetwalking prostitutes." And if one adds to this that there have been hardly any advocates of her rights or her protection, then it becomes even more intolerable.

It is hard to believe that we still condone such human-rights abuses of any part of our population. When blacks are injured or killed by police in the line of duty, great crowds storm the precinct house to expose the injustice. When gays were mistreated and attacked by police, it led to parades and protests, and a whole new movement for dignity and rights for homosexuals. This is the way public attention was focused on the legal abuse of a section of our citizenry. But every day prostitutes suffer the violation of their fundamental rights without anyone to protest the injustice and indignity.

It ought to be clear that the first and foremost reason for changing the status quo of legal sanctions against prostitutes is the denial to these women of the fundamental human rights that their personhood demands and their citizenship requires. The woman we label a prostitute has the moral right to choose her work no matter what others may think of that work. Many people don't approve of people who work at the manufacture of nuclear weapons or in industries that pollute our water and air, but people have the right to choose such occupations and professions. In this democracy we have not yet made degrading, harmful, debilitating, or dangerous work, illegal. If our freedom means anything as applied to individual rights, all women have a right to choose the work they will do!

The present law is an affront to those women and should be changed. It is a fundamental denial of a woman's right to exercise her sexual autonomy, choosing or refusing certain virtues such as romantic love or monogamous marriage or vices such as mercantile promiscuity. It should be self-evident to all but the most antilibertarian that the right to choose whether or not, or with whom, and on what terms, one will have sex is fundamental to personal autonomy and self-respect. The state has no rights in this area of individual privacy without overriding and convincing proof that exercising that autonomy is harmful to other people or to society.

But if the maltreatment and denial of freedom to the prostitute to pursue her trade were the only reasons to consider changing the law, we might never look for alternatives. However, other factors converge with women's rights at this point in history, particularly in New York City.

It is by now recognized even by the most eager antiprostitution advocate that the legalized harassment of working women is a senseless and profligate waste of time and money (supplied by public officials and taxpayers), and it is acknowledged that the use of this law in rigorous enforcement is almost completely ineffectual. If we were looking for the most glaring example of the worst cost-effective law enforcement in this nation, we would have to go no further than prostitution. The harassment and arrest of prostitutes (a simple Class B misdemeanor) leads to nothing more than revolving-door incarceration and clogged courtrooms as the criminal system grinds to a halt.

This is happening at the same time we talk of shrinking moneys, not enough police, and depleted services. We are treated by the media, daily, to accounts of lawless violence that threatens to make of us a city of frightened citizens, barricaded behind locked doors. And when the populace cries for more police protection, all we get is budgetary poor-mouthing as to why we can't have our lives and livelihoods protected. But that's not true either. It is the Mayor's Office which forces the police to make "public morality" a higher order of priority. Cleaning up Times Square seems to be more important than preventing crimes of violence against our citizens and their property. The valuable time and expertise of trained officers are wasted in hassling prostitutes, closing down massage parlors and bookstores. Haven't the politicians got their priorities all wrong? Is it more important to have Eighth Avenue look "morally respectable" than to save the lives of our elderly in the South Bronx or Sheepshead Bay? Is it more important to use police power night after night on the streets, pursuing a furtive symbol of offensive immorality, than to put those police to work preventing and intercepting violent crimes against people and property in Harlem and Bed-Stuy? It is no use arguing that we can have both. That's what budget cutting and priorities are all about. If our political leaders believe that defending "public morality" has a higher priority than reducing homicidal mortality, then we will continue to use the resources of law enforcement to play games on the street with women of the night.

What caring citizens have to ask is whether or not, in the prosecution of solicitation for prostitution, the law is caught between unreal stringency and triviality, with triviality winning the day. The whole tedious, expensive, and degrading process of enforcement activity produces very little deterrence, too few results, and not very much reform. One must wonder that though the criminal sanction is a very effective instrument for dealing with immediate harms and threats of harm, when it is turned to the enforcement of morality and acts of lesser import it seems to be a kind of law of diminishing returns in which the less threatening the conduct, the greater the social cost that enforcement seems to incur.

First we have a crime that is not even a felony and lacks a complainant. The prostitute solicits a client who has sex with her, and if no other crime occurs, he does not prefer charges against her (unless he is a "case cop"). *Two* people have engaged in lawbreaking, but neither is charging the other.

However, the prostitute is arrested (sexual discrimination), and the cost of arrest, detention, and prosecution is about $2,500 per arrest. The average number of prostitutes arrested a year is approximately twenty thousand in New York City alone. (Source: New York City Police Department.) This means a total cost of fifty million dollars a year to the public for the enforcement of a law that is probably unconstitutional and is clearly not a deterrent. One does not have to be an expert in cost-benefit analysis to see that we are engaged in law enforcement that is clearly ineffective and unduly costly.

Is there any honest politician who has the courage to call this charade what it is and stand for a more sane public response to a universal and age-old problem? The situation before us is how to redress the grievances of an abused minority with no rights and save the excessive waste of public moneys and police resources. The question before us is which way to go. One choice would be to maintain the status quo. The way things are, only perhaps more stringent: higher jail penalties, bigger fines. Last year there was a bill in committee in the New York State Legislature that called for mandatory ninety-day sentences for prostitutes convicted more than twice. (If you think the courts are backed up now, calculate what it would mean if nine out of ten prostitutes pleaded innocent and asked for a trial.) In other words, some people's answer is to do a better job cleaning the streets for a longer period of time, regardless of injustice and discrimination, even if it doesn't work.

There are some people, politicians and police commissioners, who claim that the solicitation law and the hard crackdown did stop some prostitution, particularly on Eighth Avenue, where so much money and effort were put into enforcement. But even that claim is unreal and partly dishonest, because prostitution was not stopped; it was just moved around. It's known in the jargon as "horizontal mobility" or "scatter syndrome." Through periodic crackdowns, you move the women from one precinct to another, one neighborhood to another. If one were to ask where prostitutes would congregate if there were no harassment or zoning prohibitions, the answer is: probably somewhere in the general vicinity of Times Square. This is dictated by the largest concentration of transients anywhere in the city, people coming and going at all hours of the night and day. If you add to this the observation that the large majority of recreational sex is random, unplanned activity—the train is late, the appointment is canceled, there is time to kill—it makes good sense that within walking distance of the three greatest ports (Pennsylvania Station, Port Authority Bus Terminal, and Grand Central) and the most famous object of sightseeing (Broadway and Times Square), one would find fertile ground for prostitutes.

So if we are clear that the present law doesn't work even when it is being illegally enforced, but rather results only in women being shifted around, then there is no excuse for not trying to improve on the present approach to the problem. An uninformed public, angry about other deficits in the quality of urban life, will continue to scapegoat the streetwalking prostitute. They claim that the reason our efforts to prohibit prostitution fail is our lack of will.

Many zealous antiprostitution advocates remind us that in Russia, China, and Cuba there is no prostitution, proving that the trade can be stamped out if there is a will to do so. It should be remembered that for the Marxist, prostitution is the ultimate in capitalist commercialization. In prerevolutionary Havana, gambling and prostitution were the sine qua non of American capitalist decadence and had to be stamped out. There were camps for the reeducation and retraining of prostitutes. Many Westerners who applauded this touch of morality on the part of the Communists would call the camps "brainwashing bases" if the content was political, which in fact it is. Of course, it is easier in totalitarian countries to control behavior. In Moslem countries, it is simple to curtail pickpocketing when the penalty for the crime is hand-severing. In a democracy, however, even an imperfect one, it's more difficult to enforce uniform codes of behavior. But somewhere out there, we would like to believe, there are honest politicians and sincere legislators who know the present law doesn't *work*, even if it were *not* unjust and discriminatory. It is neither morally justifiable nor cost-effective, so we should try another way.

One of the more popular alternatives being touted (by social workers, many liberal types, and even some law enforcement groups) is *legalization*. This means licensing and regulating prostitutes and the places they work. It sounds right; but as a matter of fact, it is just a fixer-upper. Is there something many people like to do that isn't good for them—like drink liquor? We'll make it O.K.—legalize it, regulate it, and tax it so that everybody benefits from it. It, too, sounds good—but good for whom, and for how long? We are told that the European model of legalization is very superior to trying to outlaw what is impossible to forbid. So a major tourist attraction in Amsterdam or Hamburg is an old-fashioned red-light district where "forbidden sex" is allowed for looking and for buying. Yes, legalization seems at first glance a progressive alternative to what we have.

But it will serve the future better to look a bit more closely at what turns out to be the state's bid to control, regulate, and collect on prostitution. In this case, the government puts all individual pimps out of business (so it would believe) and becomes the collective pimp for the whole recreational-sex industry.

It should be clear that in none of the alternatives that we look at, including the status quo, is it possible to abolish prostitution. Therefore the rationale for change must rest on other grounds. There is little question that legalization is the best known and only "tried" form of freeing prostitutes from the criminal role to which they have been assigned.

One of the questions that must be considered before turning to the practical matter of how legalization would work is a philosophical one: Should the state be involved in the regulation of private consensual sex between adults? This would appear to be a rhetorical question, yet the state has obviously in some places answered yes, for what seemed like clear and logical reasons. For example, if sex is to be accepted as a "lively commerce," then like all other trade, should it not be regulated in behalf of the "public interest"? After all, when alcohol became legal, the government had to oversee its manufacture, its bottling, its taxation, and regulate its sale both in stores and in bars. It seemed like a lot of bureaucracy and red tape; but liquor could be easily counterfeited, and the public interest must be protected. Some protection! Twenty-five thousand people a year dying from it on the highways, a million people a year dying from alcohol-related illnesses, and ten million a year sick unto death from its addicted use. Or take gambling. The state of Nevada had to regulate and control the betting game, and it's had fifty years of experience, but who would want to make a case for the fact that regulation has kept out organized crime and protected the public? It wasn't long ago that a couple of people learned how to beat the house and threatened to win as much from the casinos as the casinos fleeced from the public, and these people were barred from playing, without any protest from the Gaming Control Commission.

Our bad record at controlling and regulating what was once "sinful" and "immoral" but is now legal may not be due so much to the regulators' ineptitude as to the impossible task of controlling some things. For example, drugs, where there is so much money hardly anyone can resist being bought off; or gambling, where the profits are so incredible that "creaming" becomes a way of life.

Compared to gambling, alcohol, and cigarettes, the control

and regulation of prostitution would be far more complex, because if the state decides that it should be involved in licensing prostitutes and regulating the production and sale of recreational sex, then the question is *how* and *for whose benefit* and *by whom* it will be controlled. From the experience so far, it would seem that regulation exists for the purpose of customers. Now, since it is already clear that venereal disease and public health are not an important issue among prostitutes, that leaves out the "health issue." Unless, of course, one wants to insist that customers must also be tested for VD and carry cards verifying *they* are clean. After all, to be fair, the patron of the prostitute is just as apt to be a carrier of disease as the prostitute herself.

In the act of recreational sex, protection is a subtle and difficult question. What is the real public interest in the act of prostitution? In such a contract, is orgasm guaranteed? What is a fair price? Can the customer be required to wear condoms? What is customer satisfaction? These are the major issues over which even now there are arguments and violence, and they certainly would persist into licensing. But that's only the beginning of the difficulty, for if the state gets into regulation, it would be responsible for seeing to it that the "houses" are run well. What kind of state employees would supervise these places? Investigatory sexologists? Housing inspectors? Public health officers? What kind of regulations would be required? Would employees be required to douche before every customer? How about a mouthwash? Are employees required to remove all clothing for oral sex? Is S & M legal? Is anal sex a threat to public health and therefore "illegal" in a "legal house"? These questions may appear to be rhetorical and even ludicrous, but no more so than the question of the suitability of government being involved in such an improbable enterprise for the reason of protecting the "public interest."

We do have some experience in the licensing game, or legalization. In Europe, a number of cities (Amsterdam, Copenhagen, Stockholm, and Hamburg) have varying degrees of legalization, control, and regulation. There are stipulated places (from the harbor district in Amsterdam to the Eros Center in Hamburg) where sex is bought and sold with, if not the approval, at best the tolerance of the police and the community. In Holland the control of prostitution is maintained by designated official red-light districts and prostitutes are confined to these areas. Informal controls limit the number of prostitutes, and a working woman must be twenty-one years of age or married.

Now, one has to compare these European models with the only American experience we have with legalization—the state of Nevada. Here we have an Old West state with a high level of tolerance for illicit pleasures, especially if they can be controlled and made profitable to the government.

As has been noted previously, the law functions for the purpose of regulating the prostitute. Consequently all the restrictions are on the working woman, curtailing her freedom, and the law serves the purpose of protecting the male client and, in Nevada, the gambling industry. In other words, there is nothing wrong with a little recreational sex, provided it doesn't interfere with men gambling. Thus you make it illegal for women to solicit in casinos, and you put the brothels far enough away from gambling (a hundred miles or so) so that patrons have to drive a great distance or fly to the nearest sexual pleasure. It would be hard to imagine the Nevada law having any relevance to what legalization would look like on the Eastern Seaboard in the populous urban centers. There are probably more women working on Eleventh Avenue in Manhattan than there are in all the brothels of Nevada. Few of the latter would be willing to trade the danger and uncertainty of New York's streets for the safety of a legal "ranch" in the Southwest.

Several years ago, Arlene visited Nevada, where a paperback guide to brothels is sold along with magazines and newspapers. Most are located out in the desert, at great distances from town. They are usually converted trailers which have been connected to one another, and they are surrounded by twelve-foot-high chain-link fences which are impenetrable. Working conditions are not particularly beneficial to the women who are employed. Hired for stints of three weeks, they are not permitted to leave the premises or go to town during that period. It's a little like the days of the Old West. They are on call round the clock, and although their physical needs are well cared for (three square meals and a private room are provided), they suffer from constant boredom. Many told Arlene that they felt as if they were in jail. Management sets fees for the services they sell, and half of a woman's earnings go to the house. Several women we know have tried working there, but finding the isolation and virtual imprisonment more than they could stand, returned to New York after three weeks. So it will probably not be helpful for us to look at Nevada or Europe (except for their more relaxed attitude) for intelligent guidance on which way to go in public policy.

We stress that prohibition and legalization of prostitution are part and parcel of the same attitude toward recreational sex. Both are designed to punish and restrict women from making money on sex: in the one instance, by forbidding her activity on threat of imprisonment, and in the other, by keeping her in her place—a brothel or a special street.

If we are concerned about the human rights of working women, we have to consider the violations to these working women under any legalized or licensing system, as well as the impossible difficulties of regulating this trade. Legalization makes of the woman's choice to be a prostitute for a day, a week, or a season a label that is a permanent, legitimated stigma. Her identity could be checked by a card tied to her occupation, and would have the effect of making her stay in the life for a more prolonged period, destroying her mobility out of the occupation. The system that confines her to a "legitimate place" for selling sex also puts her under the arbitrary rules and demands of a proprietor, taking away her freedom of selection.

In legalized massage parlors or houses, she would be obliged to have sex with whoever wants her and to perform any act desired by the patron. On the street, a woman is at least free to choose her patron and establish her own limitations.

Also under a legalized system, as under prohibition, it is impossible to have nondiscriminatory laws regarding the female prostitute and the male patron—that is, unless you believe that the male patron should be licensed to buy sex in the same way the woman is licensed to sell it. What form of logic or notion of equity could justify one's being licensed without the other? The only logic is a convoluted one, composed of a discriminatory double standard and ancient practice, which will be recognized as the same one that kept women disenfranchised, underpaid, and overworked for so many years.

Before embracing the solution of legalizing prostitution as the liberal or progressive way of handling this ancient problem, we need to be reminded of that American propensity to bureaucratize and professionalize, ad infinitum, every regulated commerce that becomes a matter of law. For all legislators and politicians who are contemplating this course of licensing for prostitution, an article written a decade ago by John Beck, a graduate student at Michigan State, for the *National Review,* "The History of Legalized Prostitution, 1984–2004," should be required reading. It is a humorous but seriously critical fictitious look at what happened when the federal government decided to legalize prostitution under the Interstate Commerce Clause. Since prostitutes were clearly engaged in interstate commerce because they did not restrict their services to men who were residents of their own state, their work was legalized. Civil libertarians argued for legalization in order to expand individual liberty. Public health officials were for it so they could institute public health programs for the control of "contagious diseases." Congress saw in it the prospect of increased tax revenues.

What happens in this fictitious projection is ludicrous only in the extreme of its fantasy, but not in its particulars. A consumer-protection health measure demands that a part of each prostitute's body be stamped with the seal "HEW inspected," which prostitutes complain mars the beauty of their bodies. Then there is the prostitutes' battle for coverage by the minimum wage law and unemployment compensation. This is followed by a struggle to organize an American Prostitutes Association, which passes licensing laws for controlling the quality of new entrants into the profession. Discrimination among prostitutes (gentlemen *do* prefer blondes!) leads to the Equal Opportunities Act, providing uniform pricing and requiring that contracts for prostitution service be made sight unseen. Inequality among customers arises when many poor unmarried males cannot afford to pay prostitutes, and since clearly sex is as much a necessity as food, housing, and medicine, Congress adopts the Sex Stamps program for needy males.

This humorous projection of legalized recreational sex is frightening in its logical depiction of reality. The baggage that legalized licensing carries with it is heavy indeed. More important, no compelling case can be made for legalization in light of the burdens it would bring to governmental institutions.

Now, if not legalization, and not the status quo, what then? Initially, from the vantage point of our work, it would appear that the most important step to redress the grievances and correct the wrongs done to streetwalking prostitutes is the simple act of *decriminalization*—through repeal of all laws which regulate sex between consenting adults, regardless of the form it takes or whether money changes hands. That repeal alone would, for the first time, grant to thousands of women a freedom of choice and an autonomy in regard to the work they choose, and entitle them to equal concern and respect. It would restore equality and justice for a large number of working women, delivering them from persecution, prosecution, and imprisonment for engaging in recreational sex.

For those to whom "principles" are not so important, who prefer to deal with quantum ethics—what is right or just is not as important as how many are affected—the statistics for prostitutes, given the nature of the illicit trade, are not too precise. However, a conservative estimate is that there are in the United States approximately 500,000 full-time women in the field of recreational sex and as many more who work part-time or occasionally. Since prostitution has been growing in the last several decades and the turnover is fairly predictable, it can be estimated that women who are or have been engaged in prostitution at some time in their lives numbers some five million.

It should be clear that this act of repeal, though it will be a correct and courageous one on the part of our legislators, will not stop prostitution any more than criminalization stopped it, but it will help set the record straight on the injustice toward women in our society. It may be that in order to correct other community problems that are alleged to occur when women solicit for sex, we will need to experiment with social means apart from criminal violations—such actions as "geographical and time zoning," which the police have already tried (it is claimed with some success) under the present prohibitory system.

Perhaps a word is in order here to address the concerns and complaints of people who care about the rights of the women but have priorities about the practice of prostitution in their residential neighborhoods. The first fact that ought to be reiterated is that prostitutes do not want or choose to be in residential areas, but they are driven there by police who have been given orders to evacuate them, for example, from Times Square or midtown Lexington Avenue. If some consensus could be reached about areas out of residential locales that are not dark, dangerous, and uninhabited, then it is entirely possible that a trade-off for decriminalization might be the authorization of designated areas of town in which the women could work without excessive harassment. Or to put it negatively, there might be "off limits" designations for prostitution, much like areas where trucks can't go or parking is not allowed. This method does not mean a "combat zone," as in the Boston experiment. One of the complaints that citizens lodge about the practice of prostitution is that it turns any place into a sordid and ugly area, unsafe and with many criminal elements. The proof offered for this is Times Square, where drug merchants, muggers, and street hustlers congregate. It is faulty logic and a bad example. For example, Park and Lexington avenues between Twenty-ninth and Twenty-third streets is a bustling business district by day, interspersed with condominiums and apartment houses. It is neither unsafe nor is there a high incidence of crime. The major complaint of residents is that in the evening there is public sex in automobiles or on stoops, much of which is allied with having no place to go for sex—hotels are periodically harassed and closed down. Perhaps large parking lots closed at night could be utilized for "car trick" prostitutes to prevent public acts of sex.

Another form of containment, without legalized brothels, could be some kind of "time zoning," where given areas would be "on limits" to street prostitution at certain times of day or night. Since many of the charges against the present situation seem to be that people say they would rather not *see* prostitutes, perhaps working women could be allowed in an area only during hours when people are not normally on the streets. (There is no guarantee that it would be 100 percent effective any more than no-parking zones and restricted speeds and red lights are for motorists.)

Though the proponents of decriminalization cannot honestly claim that it will abolish prostitution, they do assert that, in addition to the granting of long overdue justice to this class of working women, there will be benefits to the larger community. For the law enforcement establishment, it will lift the stigma of the police as enforcers of morality having to pose as tricks, entrapping women and chasing them down the streets in arbitrary and illegal street sweeps. Hundreds of policemen will be freed to do what they are trained and disciplined to do —prevent real crimes against persons and property.

The courts, which are now the clogged obstacle in the channel of achieving a quick and speedy trial, will be relieved of repetitious and noneffective prosecution of working women in a revolving-door scandal at a time when serious crimes and their solutions are appallingly postponed. As recently as last year, the courts in New York City were practically paralyzed by an overload that saw people locked up for six months when trials were postponed.

It is our belief that the time has come for us to look at this social problem without the heat of emotions that it seems to elicit, and to apply some historical lessons and studied reasonableness to an issue that most people believe is one of public nuisance, or "street aesthetics." They think that for the sake of our urban quality of life, prostitution must be abolished. It is not that simple, and we can no longer pretend that there is not present here also a historical injustice against women that resembles a larger pattern of discrimination and inequity.

Almost twenty years ago, we spent much of our time learning about and counseling women from another "illicit underworld" —those who sought illegal abortions. They were invisible women, either ignored, pitied, or whispered about, but for the most part they were unknown to most of us, hidden from our sight, suffering silently and profoundly, paying an excessive penalty for the desire to be free from state-imposed, mandatory childbearing. When the light finally shone upon this dark side of society's primitive and cruel treatment, we saw that these women were our mothers, our sisters, our daughters.

It will be different regarding the matter of prostitution someday, when our ignorance is overcome by enlightenment, when our prejudice gives way to knowledge, our repulsion is replaced by compassion; then the prostitute will become a human being. When that time comes, her work will be seen for what it is—

hard, physical, demeaning, like so many jobs in our industrial society. Then we will find that her life is not too different from our own, and her children, in need of more love, time, and attention from their mother, are just like so many children in our society.

When that time comes, and this "alien woman" is recognized as part of our humanity, then we will know that what we have done to her is "cruel and unusual punishment."

The cold December rain with its winter rawness made the night feel colder than usual. The streets where the women work were emptier than usual. It was Christmas Eve, and the prostitutes knew from experience it would not be a night of financial rewards, and the occasion seemed to evoke in the women a bittersweet note: resentment that they were out there with little hope of success, and happiness that tomorrow would be Christmas. As they talked in the warmth of the bus, sipping spiked eggnog, our holiday treat, they seemed fatalistic about the missing tricks who would be with their families, and had spent all their money on gifts. But there was something else in the air that night. There appeared on the bus a prostitute we had not seen before. She was a tall, statuesque ebony woman, with beautiful eyes and smile. It was as though the miserable street and the hard time was not there, as she spoke with a kind of glow about being home on Christmas Day in Philadelphia with her seven brothers and sisters. It was a tradition as warm and real for her as the "mean streets" from which she wrung her living. She spoke of the gifts she would bring for all the small ones, and her eyes beamed.

It was that night we announced for the first time that we had written a book about them, their lives and their work. We said we hoped that it might make those outside their world understand them better. The women hardly contained their elation, and expressed their surprise and happiness that anyone should give them a good review. Finally one of the women spoke, out

of the experience of a lot of broken dreams and disappoint-
ments, and asked, "Do you really think it will make any difference?"

As the women left the bus that night to return to the empty
stroll with calls of "Merry Christmas," we were suddenly alone.
We didn't speak, but that last question remained there in the
silence of our thoughts.

Street Prostitution Glossary

bitch: word used affectionately by prostitutes to describe their co-workers

blow job: fellatio; genital-oral sex

bottom woman: one who has been with a particular pimp the longest and in whom he has the most confidence

break luck: the first date a prostitute turns on a night-long tour

car tricks: customers who choose to receive sexual services in their automobiles

case cop: plainclothes police officer whose job is to arrest women for solicitation as opposed to loitering

doing a blow: snorting or base-lining cocaine

fence: one who has stolen goods for sale

flatbacking: engaging in conventional intercourse

hand job: the least expensive sexual service

ho: street slang for whore, prostitute

hooker: prostitute; working woman; call girl

hot sheet hotel: small, usually run-down hostelry which caters almost exclusively to street prostitutes and their customers

my man: my pimp

my people: my pimp

nigger: a prostitute's man—not a racial epithet

outlaw: a prostitute living and working without a pimp

pimp squad: police department's special unit to find and arrest pimps

player: pimp

regulars: tricks who come to a particular prostitute periodically

righteous arrest: the opposite of an illegal arrest

rolling a trick: stealing (usually money or credit cards) from a customer

rubber man: person who sells prophylactics to women on the street

sportin' life: the world of the pimp

square up: leave the life of prostitution

square world: the world of middle-class culture

stroll: the street territory on which streetwalkers ply their trade

trap: money a woman has made on a given shift

trick: male customer of prostitutes; also called john and date

turn-out: someone who recently became a prostitute

wife-in-law: relationship of several women with the same pimp